English Paper Piecing II

Vicki Bellino

Dedication

To Madilyn, Lexi, Ava, and Olyvia... my constant source of love, joy, and inspiration.

Acknowledgments

A design can only be as appealing as the fabrics used to make the project, so I thank Marcus Fabrics, Riley Blake, and Moda for contributing beautiful fabrics that I used to create the projects shown in this book.

Without precut paper pieces, there would be no book, so my heartfelt thanks and gratitude go to JoAnn at Paper Pieces for providing me with all of my paper pieces, as well as creating new shapes specifically for use in this book.

English Paper Piecing II
© 2014 by Vicki Bellino

Martingale®
19021 120th Ave. NE, Ste. 102
Bothell, WA 98011-9511 USA
ShopMartingale.com

No part of this product may be reproduced in any form, unless otherwise stated, in which case reproduction is limited to the use of the purchaser. The written instructions, photographs, designs, projects, and patterns are intended for the personal, noncommercial use of the retail purchaser and are under federal copyright laws; they are not to be reproduced by any electronic, mechanical, or other means, including informational storage or retrieval systems, for commercial use. Permission is granted to photocopy patterns for the personal use of the retail purchaser. Attention teachers: Martingale encourages you to use this book for teaching, subject to the restrictions stated above.

The information in this book is presented in good faith, but no warranty is given nor results guaranteed. Since Martingale has no control over choice of materials or procedures, the company assumes no responsibility for the use of this information.

Printed in China
19 18 17 16 15 14   8 7 6 5 4 3 2 1

Library of Congress Cataloging-in-Publication Data is available upon request.

ISBN: 978-1-60468-365-3

Mission Statement

Dedicated to providing quality products and service to inspire creativity.

Credits

PRESIDENT AND CEO: Tom Wierzbicki
EDITOR IN CHIEF: Mary V. Green
DESIGN DIRECTOR: Paula Schlosser
MANAGING EDITOR: Karen Costello Soltys
ACQUISITIONS EDITOR: Karen M. Burns
TECHNICAL EDITOR: Ellen Pahl
COPY EDITOR: Melissa Bryan
PRODUCTION MANAGER: Regina Girard
COVER DESIGNER: Regina Girard
INTERIOR DESIGNER: Regina Girard
PHOTOGRAPHER: Brent Kane
ILLUSTRATOR: Missy Shepler

Contents

Introduction	4
English Paper Piecing	5
Quiltmaking Basics	9
Topiary	14
Simple Splendor	21
Cover-Up Duo	26
Small/Medium	27
Medium/Large	30
Little Dresden Patch	33
In Full Bloom	36
Fig Tree Flowers	40
Summer Garden Bed Runner	46
Just Judie Goes Miniature	50
Flower Garden Tote	55
Indigo Stars	59
About the Author	64

Introduction

I can't begin to tell you how thrilled I was when Martingale asked me to write a follow-up to my book *English Paper Piecing: Fresh New Quilts from Bloom Creek* (Martingale, 2012). My passion for English paper piecing continues to grow, and I'm glad that others feel the same way!

As I began to gather my thoughts for the content of this book, there were two things I knew for sure. The first was that I wanted to include projects that would appeal to paper piecers of all levels: some ambitious projects that take more time to complete, as well as simpler projects with the beginning English paper piecer in mind. Second, I wanted to use a variety of shapes—many of which weren't introduced in my first book on English paper piecing—to make an assortment of projects, from a tote to sewing-machine covers to wall hangings to quilts.

I hope you will find English paper piecing as enjoyable as I do!

English Paper Piecing

English paper piecing dates back to at least the early 1700s. It is a time-honored method of piecing that uses paper templates cut to the exact finished size. These templates are used as a guide for both cutting and piecing. Fabric is basted to the paper pieces, and the paper serves as a stabilizer, eliminating any stretching or distortion along bias edges. The paper remains in place until units are complete, guaranteeing that the pieces are accurate and will fit together perfectly.

As with many quilting techniques, there are several ways to do English paper piecing and a variety of supplies to choose from. The instructions that follow are for the method I prefer. For each project in this book, I've provided a pattern for cutting your own paper pieces. However, I find that for a relatively small monetary investment, purchasing precut paper pieces is the way to go. It eliminates the time involved in tracing and cutting, and the paper pieces can be reused several times, thereby giving you more bang for your buck. For all of the patterns in this book, precut paper pieces are available at www.paperpieces.com. Many quilt shops also carry paper templates for English paper piecing. Note that the sizes given for the paper pieces in the materials lists refer to the length of one side of the shape. For example, a 1" hexagon measures 1" along each side.

MAKING YOUR OWN PAPER PIECES

All you will need to make your own paper pieces are template plastic and heavyweight paper.

1. Trace the original pattern very carefully onto template plastic and cut it out to make an accurate master template.
2. Trace around the master template onto the paper as many times as instructed for your project, and carefully cut out each piece just inside the traced line.

   Your templates may be slightly less accurate than purchased die-cut pieces, but if you always use the master template for tracing, and cut carefully, they should work just fine. As with purchased paper pieces, you can save them and reuse them several times.

Cutting

The method for cutting paper pieces is the same for all shapes. Place the paper shape onto the wrong side of your fabric and pin in place. Use scissors to cut out the fabric shape a generous ¼" beyond the paper piece. An exact ¼" seam allowance isn't necessary.

PIN OR PEN

A glue pen, available from companies such as Sewline and Fons & Porter, is a great tool for keeping the paper in place throughout the cutting and basting process. It's especially helpful when working with very small pieces, and the paper will already be in position for basting.

For a speedier method, use a rotary cutter to cut your fabric into squares or strips that are a generous ½" larger than the shape you're using. This makes the cutting go much faster. You will have more fabric on the wrong side of the paper piece, but this won't show when the quilt is assembled.

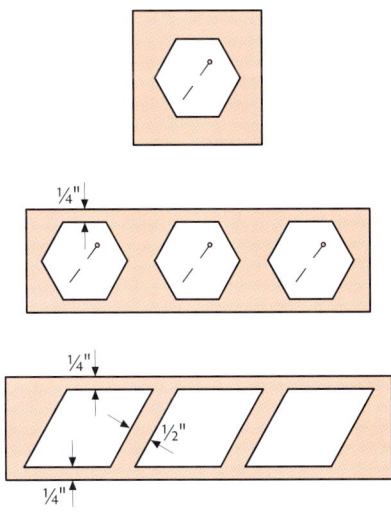

When cutting scallops, do not add a seam allowance at the bottom straight edge, but rather, cut the fabric even with the straight edge of the paper. This will allow you to more accurately align the bottom straight edge of the scallop with the straight edge of your quilt block or border.

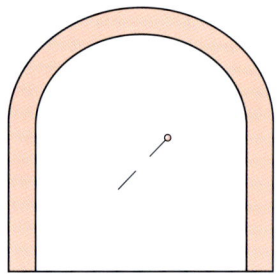

You will notice that I often "fussy cut" prints for various designs throughout the projects. This is easy to do by placing the paper template over the area in the print that you want to feature, and then cutting out your shape with scissors.

Basting

After cutting, you'll fold the fabric seam allowances over the paper templates and baste them to the paper. This makes a precise finished-size shape, with no worries about that exact ¼" seam allowance. Each piece will be stabilized and ready to sew to other shapes.

1. Thread a size 7, 8, or 9 Sharp needle with thread that contrasts with the fabric. This will make the basting much easier to see when you're ready to remove it. Knot the end.

> **EMPTY THOSE SPOOLS**
> This is a good time to use up thread you wouldn't normally use for piecing, or thread you'd like to get rid of, as it will eventually be removed and discarded.

2. Center the paper template over the fabric and pin in place. You can also use a small swipe of a water-soluble glue pen to hold the paper in place. This works well for very small pieces, and if you used it during the cutting step, your pieces will already be in position for basting.

3. Fold the seam allowance over the shape, and bring the needle up through the fabric and paper with the knot on the right side. Baste through the fabric and paper with long stitches.

4. Continue folding the fabric over the edges on all sides, basting through the fabric and paper with long stitches.

5. When you reach the point where you started, cut the thread, leaving about a 1" tail. It isn't necessary to tie a knot at the end of the basting.

Hexagons

The hexagon is probably the most popular and well-known shape that quilters associate with English paper piecing. It is also one of the easiest shapes to work with.

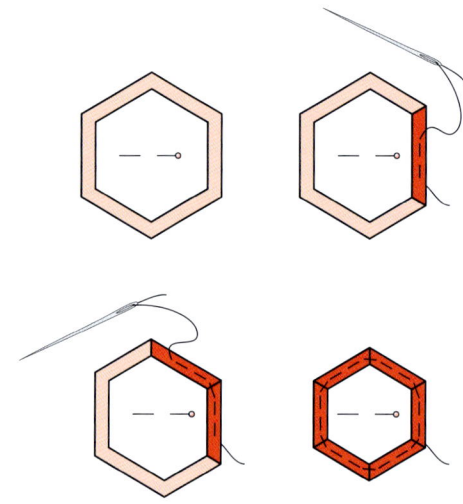

Points

Flower petals, diamonds, and leaves all involve stitching points.

When basting diamonds, baste the wider angles by creating a small fold or pleat in the seam allowance. For the narrow points, think about where the sharp, angled points will be. If they will not be on the outside, you can let the "tails wag." This means it is not necessary for you to fold the fabric over to a sharp point. When whipstitched together, these inner points will overlap, creating a nice finished center.

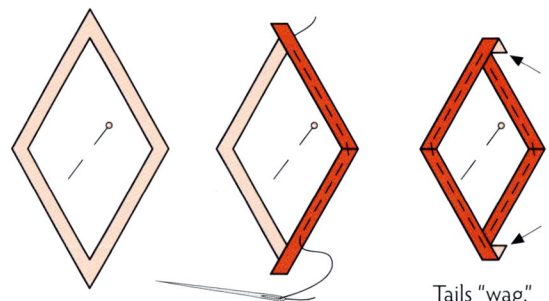

Tails "wag."

English Paper Piecing II

For a design such as a flower or diamond starflower, let the tails wag on the interior points, but fold over and baste a sharp point on the outer points. If you choose to hand appliqué your flower to a background, you can let both tails wag and simply tuck under the outer tail with your appliqué needle. For a leaf shape or a diamond that is appliquéd as a single diamond, you will need to fold over and baste a sharp point on each end.

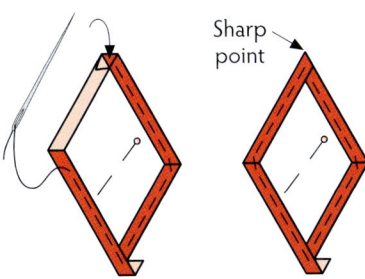

Curves

English paper piecing works well for curves too. Dresden petals, leaves, scallops, and circles all have curved edges. When basting a curved piece such as a Dresden petal or scallop, start at the bottom of one long side and baste up the side to the curve. As you fold over the seam allowance around the curve, ease in fullness and take smaller basting stitches. Baste circles in the same manner, beginning anywhere along the curve.

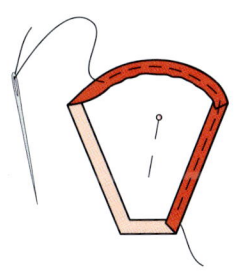

Whipstitching

Once you've basted your fabric to the paper pieces, it's time to whipstitch the pieces together. This step is the same regardless of the shapes you're using. I've tried a variety of threads for whipstitching, but ultimately I've found that a 40-weight machine-piecing thread or a 60-weight appliqué thread works best.

Hexagons

With two hexagons right sides together and using thread to match or blend well with your fabric, take a small stitch just catching the folded edges of the fabric. To minimize the thread showing on the right side of your paper pieces, keep your stitches close together. When you reach the end, add the next hexagon piece and continue whipstitching.

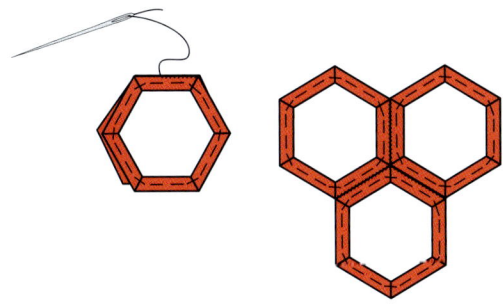

Diamonds

Align two diamonds with right sides together and whipstitch toward the center point. Once you reach the point of the tail, open up the two diamonds, and then

DRESDEN PETALS AND DRESDEN BLADES

These pieces are very similar, the only difference being that the ends of Dresden petals are rounded and the ends of Dresden blades are pointed. If you are purchasing precut paper shapes from Paper Pieces, the plates formed by pointed shapes are called Chrysanthemums.

When basting these pieces, it isn't necessary to fold over the seam allowance and baste the short bottom end. Just cut the fabric 1/8" to 1/4" beyond the paper and leave a raw edge.

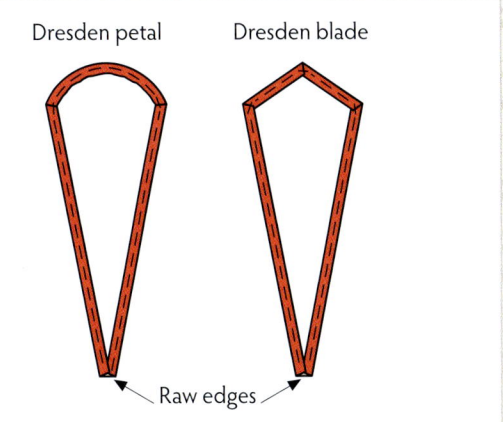

add the next one, whipstitching from the center tail to the outer edge.

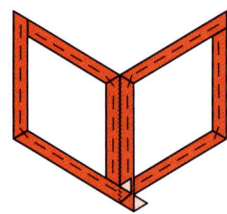

Dresden Blades or Petals

With right sides together, align two Dresden pieces along the straight edges. Begin at the bottom of one long side and whipstitch toward the curve or point. When you reach the beginning of the curve or point, knot and cut the thread. Open up the pieces and whipstitch the next piece in the same manner. Continue adding pieces until the Dresden plate or flower is complete.

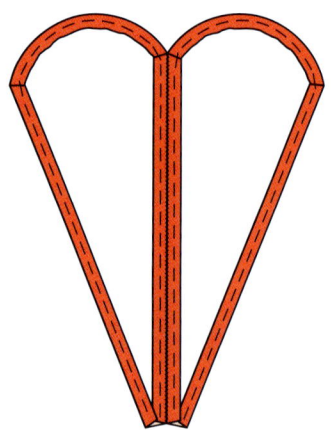

Flower Petals

Align two petals right sides together and whipstitch from the center point upward to join the edges. When the pieces begin to curve away, stop stitching, knot and cut the thread. Open up the pieces and add the next petal. Continue in this manner until the flower is whipstitched together.

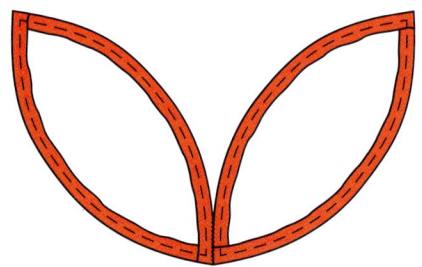

Scallops

With right sides together, align two scallop pieces along the straight edges. Begin at the bottom straight edge and whipstitch toward the curve. When you reach the beginning of the curve, knot and cut the thread. Continue adding scallops as directed in the project.

Finishing

If you're making a design that will be appliquéd to a quilt block, such as a hexagon or a diamond flower, leave the basting stitches and paper pieces in place until all of the pieces are whipstitched together. Then press the unit well on both sides, remove the basting thread, and pop out the paper pieces.

> **SPRAY FIRST**
>
> I like to use a spritz of spray sizing before pressing and removing the paper. This keeps the seam allowance in place nicely and makes it easier to appliqué to the block. Lightly spritz both the right side and the wrong side of the piece. Remember to save your paper pieces as they can be reused several times.

Another option when appliquéing English paper-pieced units to a block is to press well on both sides, and then remove the basting thread only. Hand or machine appliqué the unit to the block, cut away the fabric on the back under the appliqué, and then pop out the paper pieces. Try both methods to see which you prefer.

When making a quilt or other project that is almost entirely English paper pieced (such as "Fig Tree Flowers" on page 40), don't remove the basting or the paper pieces until all sides of a block have been whipstitched. Leave the basting stitches and paper pieces in place around the outer edges of the blocks or units until the quilt center has been assembled.

Quiltmaking Basics

The projects in this book use not only the English-paper-piecing technique but also machine piecing and hand or machine appliqué. I'll share the techniques that work best for me, but if you prefer a different method to achieve the same result, use it! Regardless of what technique you choose, accurate cutting and piecing are key to success. All of the piecing in this book is based on an accurate ¼" seam allowance unless otherwise indicated.

Freezer-Paper Appliqué

This method results in appliqué pieces with turned-under, finished edges. The pieces can be either hand or machine stitched in place on the block or quilt. *Note: For several projects in this book that involved leaves and circles, I basted my fabric to precut paper pieces rather than using freezer-paper templates to prepare my pieces. Use whichever method you prefer.*

Preparing the Appliqués

For this method of appliqué, you'll need to cut a freezer-paper template for each piece needed. For example, if your project has eight leaves, you'll need to cut eight leaves out of freezer paper.

1. Trace the appliqué patterns onto the non-shiny side of freezer paper. Using scissors for cutting paper, cut out each shape on the traced line.

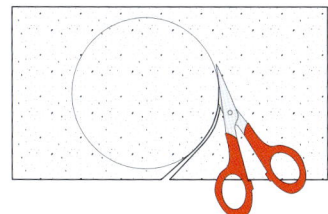

2. Iron the freezer-paper templates, shiny side down, onto the right side of the chosen appliqué fabric. Cut out each piece, adding a ¼" seam allowance around the entire shape. *Note: For small pieces or those with points, a slightly smaller seam allowance of ⅛" to 3⁄16" will work best.*

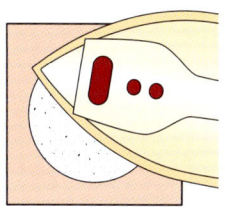 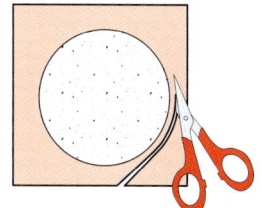

3. Carefully peel off the freezer-paper template. Turn the fabric piece over so that the wrong side is facing up. Center the freezer-paper template, shiny side up, on top of the fabric, with the ⅛" to ¼" seam allowance all around. Using a small iron and working on a smooth, firm surface, iron the seam allowance over the edge of the freezer-paper template.

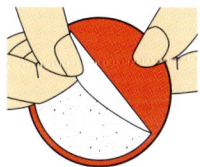 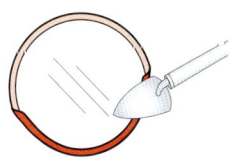

4. On the wrong side of the shape, apply a few small dots of appliqué glue to the seam allowance and gently finger-press the shape into position on your block or quilt, leaving the freezer paper in place.

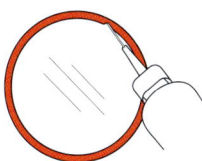

5. Stitch in place by hand or machine.

Stitching by Machine

To machine stitch the appliqué pieces in place, you have several options for both the thread and the stitch. If you don't want the thread to show, use a lightweight monofilament (clear for light fabrics and smoke for dark) and a 60/8 machine needle. Or, you can use a fine, lightweight thread that matches the color of the appliqué fabric and a 70/10 machine needle. Use an open-toe presser foot for good visibility and set your machine to a blind hem stitch, or a stitch similar to the one circled below. This will result in nearly invisible stitching. You can also use a small zigzag stitch, blanket stitch, or other decorative stitch if you want the stitching to be part of the design.

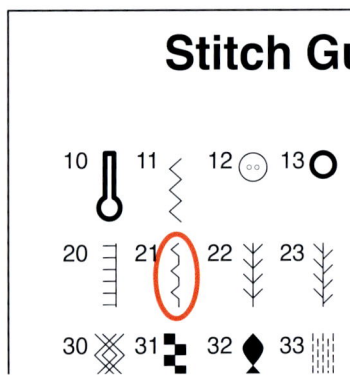

1. Begin stitching by using a straight stitch, and take a few very short stitches to anchor the thread. Change to your chosen stitch and sew around the shape carefully, slowly turning the shape as you stitch around the curves. To pivot at corners and points, stop with the needle in the down position, lift the presser foot, and turn the appliqué piece. Do this when the needle is along the outer edge in the background fabric, not in the appliqué fabric. When you reach the starting point, change to a straight stitch and take a few short tacking stitches or backstitches to anchor the thread. Clip the threads and remove your work from the machine.

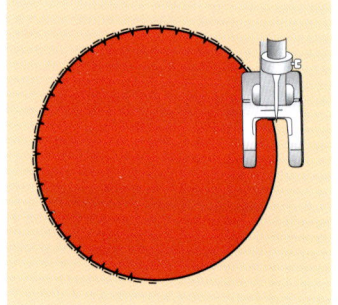

2. Turn the quilt or block over and cut away the fabric inside of the appliqué stitching, leaving a ¼" seam allowance. Remove the paper. Press the piece gently from the right side.

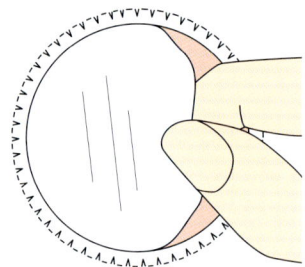

Stitching by Hand

Use an appliqué needle and thread that matches the appliqué fabric. Because the edges are already turned under, hand appliqué will be easy and relaxing.

1. Knot the thread and bring the needle up through the edge of the appliqué shape. Insert the needle into the background fabric right next to the appliqué and bring it back up about 1⁄16" to 1⁄8" away, catching just a few threads along the folded edge of the appliqué shape. Continue around the shape until you reach the beginning stitch.

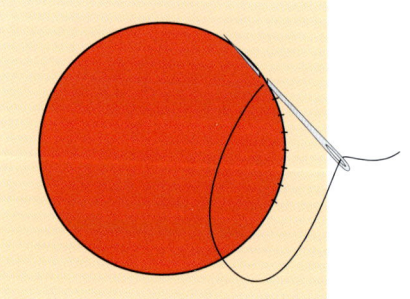

2. Knot the thread on the wrong side of the fabric and follow step 2 of "Stitching by Machine" above to complete the block.

Fusible Appliqué

This method results in a raw edge that's finished with machine stitching. There are many different fusible webs on the market, but I find that a lightweight product works the best. General instructions are provided here, but be sure to read the manufacturer's instructions beforehand for the product you use. This method is fast, but when tracing onto the fusible web, you'll need to reverse any nonsymmetrical appliqué patterns if they're not already reversed.

1. Trace the appliqué patterns onto the paper side of the fusible web.

2. Cut out the shapes approximately ¼" beyond the traced lines. For larger pieces, I use the "windowpane" technique and cut away the fusible web in the center, leaving approximately ¼" of web inside the traced line. This prevents stiffness and keeps the appliqués soft and flexible because they're not fused in the center.

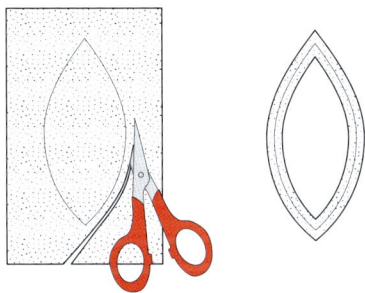

3. With the fusible side down and following the manufacturer's instructions, iron the fusible web onto the *wrong side* of the appliqué fabric. Cut out each piece on the traced lines.

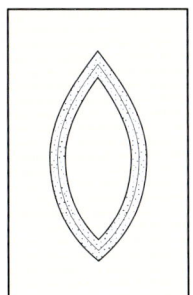 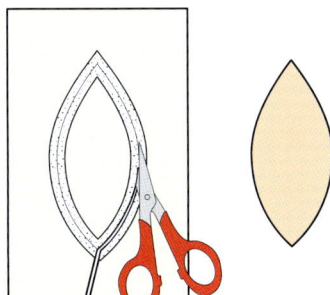

4. Remove the paper, position the appliqué pieces onto the block (or quilt), and iron in place, following the manufacturer's instructions. Machine stitch around the raw edges with a blanket stitch, satin stitch, or invisible stitch as described in "Stitching by Machine" on page 9.

Making Bias Vines

There are several different methods for making bias vines, but the following method is the one I find to be the easiest.

1. Open up the fabric so that it has no fold. Position the 45° line of an acrylic ruler on one selvage edge. Using a rotary cutter, cut along the long edge of the acrylic ruler. Move the ruler over to the desired width of the bias strip and make another cut. Continue in this manner until you've cut the required number of strips.

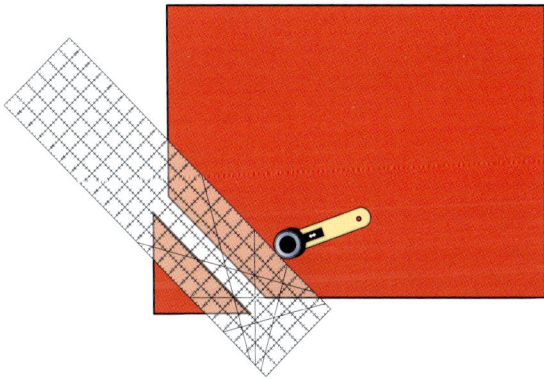

2. Sew the strips together end to end to make one long bias strip. To do this, place strips right sides together, offsetting the ends by ¼". Sew at a 45° angle, trim the points, and press the seam allowances open.

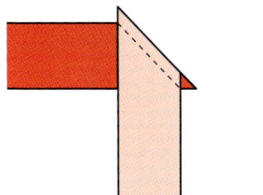 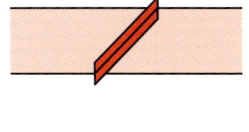

Quiltmaking Basics 11

3. Fold the bias strip in half with *wrong sides* together and press. Sew ¼" from the raw edge along the entire length of the strip to make a tube.

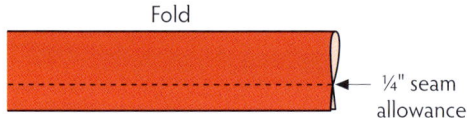

4. Working on your ironing surface, insert a bias press bar (metal or plastic) into the bias tube and roll the seam allowance to the top when moving the bias bar through the tube. Press well as you move the bias bar through the tube, pressing the seam allowances to the side. Continue until the entire tube has been pressed. (Spray sizing is helpful when pressing.) Remove the bias bar.

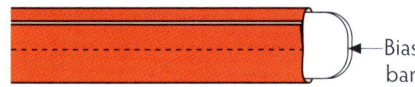

5. Use dots of appliqué glue to position the vine on the quilt top. Appliqué by hand or machine using a blind stitch, blanket stitch, or small zigzag stitch.

> **NARROW VINES**
> If the bias vines are very narrow, trim the seam allowances after sewing the tube to keep them from showing.

Preparing for Machine Quilting

I machine quilt most of my own projects and will share the steps I use to prepare a quilt top for machine quilting. If you send your quilts out to be machine quilted, be sure to check with the quilter to determine how much larger than the quilt top the backing fabric and batting should be.

1. Mark the quilting design onto the right side of the finished quilt top, being sure to use a water-soluble marking pen or pencil. An assortment of these can be found at your local quilt shop.

2. Prepare the backing fabric. If your quilt is large, you'll have to piece the backing fabric together widthwise or lengthwise in order to cut a piece approximately 4" larger than the quilt top. I press the seam allowances to one side.

3. Lay the backing fabric on a hard, flat surface (such as a table) with the wrong side facing up. Smooth the fabric out until it's taut (but not stretched) and use tape or binder clips to fasten it in place. Lay the batting on top, smoothing it out but not stretching it. Lay the quilt on top of the batting, centering it on the batting and backing fabric.

4. Pin through all layers using safety pins, spacing them approximately 4" apart over the entire quilt.

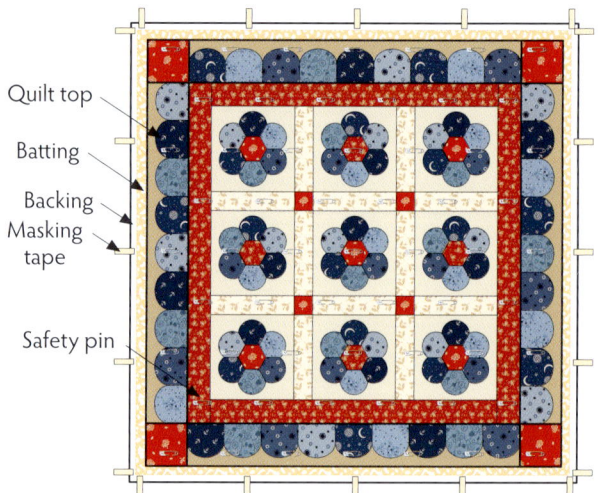

5. Quilt as desired. For machine quilting straight lines, or for stitching in the ditch, it's helpful to use a walking foot. For free-motion quilting, drop your sewing machine's feed dogs and attach the darning foot; this will allow you to quilt curved designs such as stippling or feathers.

6. When you've finished machine quilting and removed the safety pins, spread the quilt out flat on the floor and spray it with water to remove the markings of your quilt design. Don't attempt to remove the markings in the washing machine before you sew on the binding!

7. After the quilt is dry, trim the batting and backing even with the quilt top and square up the corners.

Making a Hanging Sleeve

I recommend making a hanging sleeve for every project. It takes very little time and is much easier to sew onto the quilt as you're finishing it, rather than later on down the road. You never know when you might decide to enter your creation into a quilt show or take it off the bed and hang it on the wall.

1. Cut a 7"-wide strip of backing fabric the length of the top edge of the quilt, minus 2". Double fold a ½" hem at each end and stitch in place. Press the strip in half lengthwise with wrong sides together, aligning the raw edges.
2. On the back of the quilt, center and align the raw edges of the sleeve along the top edge of the quilt. Pin or baste in place.
3. Sew the binding to the quilt, and then whipstitch the folded edge of the sleeve to the backing fabric.

Binding the Quilt

All of the quilts in this book call for binding strips that are cut 2" wide, which is the narrow binding I like for most projects. If you prefer a wider binding, feel free to cut your strips 2¼" or 2½" wide. The yardage requirements given with each project should be enough to accommodate wider strips. Measure the entire perimeter of the quilt and add about 10". Divide this number by 40" to get the number of binding strips you will need to cut for your quilt.

1. Sew together binding strips end to end at a 45° angle, trim, and press the seam allowances open. Cut one end of this long binding strip at a 45° angle, fold over ¼", and press. Fold the long binding strip in half lengthwise, wrong sides together, and press.

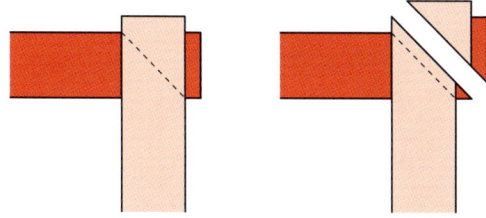

2. Align the raw edges of the binding strip with the raw edges of the quilt top, beginning with the 45° end of the binding strip. Using a ¼" seam allowance, begin sewing approximately 4" from the end of the binding strip and continue until you're ¼" from the corner. Stop stitching and remove the quilt from the machine.

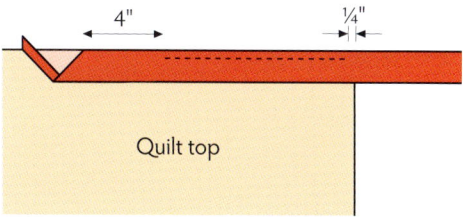

3. Fold the binding up as shown to create a 45° angle. Then fold the binding down to align the raw edges with the next side of the quilt. Begin sewing at the fold and continue to the next corner. Repeat the mitering process at each corner.

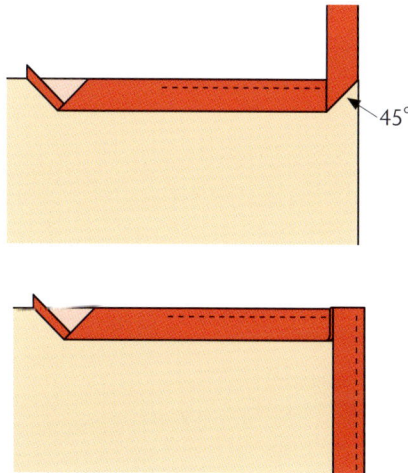

4. When you're nearing the binding tail where you started, trim the binding strip at a 45° angle so that the end of the binding will overlap the beginning of the binding by 2". Tuck the newly trimmed end into the turned-under end, align the raw edges, and continue sewing until you've stitched over the first few stitches.

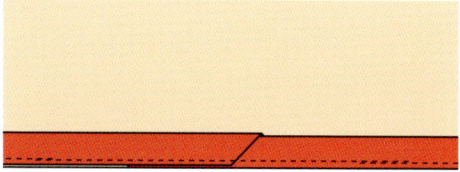

5. Turn the folded edge of the binding over the seam allowance to the back of the quilt and stitch in place by hand.

Topiary

I had the pleasure of visiting a fabulous home-and-garden store during a trip to Washington state. This store had the most beautiful topiaries in very unusual pots. I was immediately inspired and began designing my own Dresden topiary while on a quilt retreat with some of my favorite quilting friends. For me, inspiration often comes while sharing great company in a relaxed, fun environment!

FINISHED WALL HANGING: 20½" x 44½"

Materials

Yardage is based on 42"-wide fabric.
½ yard of black print for appliqués, inner border, corner squares, and binding
⅜ yard of floral for outer border
1 fat quarter *each* of 2 small-scale light prints for background
1 fat quarter of black tone on tone for vase and handles
1 fat eighth *each* of 4 assorted red prints for appliqués
1 fat eighth *each* of 4 assorted green prints for appliqués
5" x 5" piece of brown print for stems
1½ yards of fabric for backing
25" x 49" piece of batting
16 large Dresden petal papers, 3 11/16"
12 medium Dresden petal papers, 1⅞"
8 small Dresden petal papers, 13/16"
1 hexagon paper, 1¼"
1 hexagon paper, 1"
8 hexagon papers, ¾"
Size 7, 8, or 9 Sharp needle and thread to match fabric
Appliqué glue and freezer paper **OR** ⅓ yard of lightweight fusible web, 18" wide

Cutting

Refer to "English Paper Piecing" on page 5 for cutting hexagons and Dresden petals; baste all shapes to the papers. Refer to "Quiltmaking Basics" on page 9 to prepare the vase, handles, and stems for appliqué. Patterns are on pages 17–20.

From 1 light print, cut:
14 squares, 4½" x 4½"

From the second light print, cut:
13 squares, 4½" x 4½"

From the 8 assorted prints, cut a *total* of:
16 large Dresden petals (2 from each)
6 red medium Dresden petals
6 green medium Dresden petals
4 red small Dresden petals
4 green small Dresden petals
4 red hexagons, ¾"
3 green hexagons, ¾"

From the black tone on tone, cut:
1 vase
1 handle and 1 handle reversed

From the black print, cut:
1 hexagon, ¾"
1 hexagon, 1"
1 hexagon, 1¼"
3 strips, 1½" x 42"; crosscut into 2 strips, 1½" x 12½", and 2 strips, 1½" x 38½"
4 squares, 3½" x 3½"
4 strips, 2" x 42"

From the brown print, cut:
3 stems

From the floral, cut:
3 strips, 3½" x 42"; crosscut into 2 strips, 3½" x 14½", and 2 strips, 3½" x 38½"

Making the Wall Hanging

1. Arrange the 4½" light squares in nine rows of three squares each, alternating the prints. Sew the squares together in rows, pressing seam allowances as shown. Sew the rows together to make the background. It should measure 12½" x 36½".

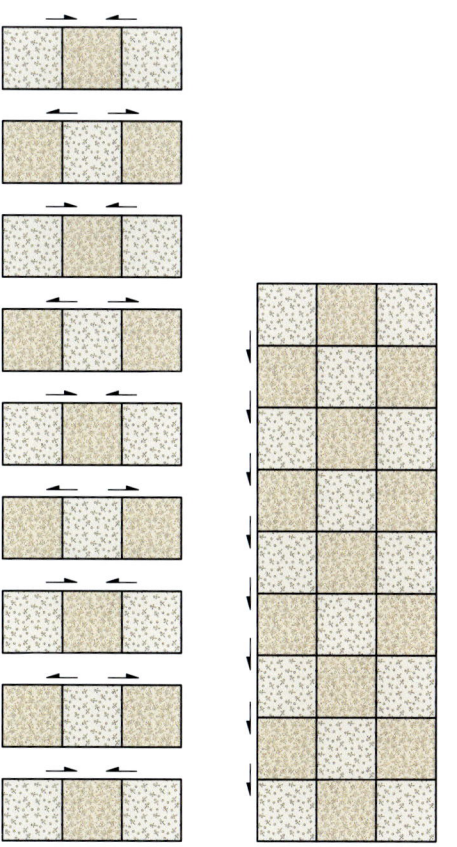

Topiary 15

2. Alternating four red and four green small Dresden petals, whipstitch them together to form a small Dresden flower. Press well on both sides; remove basting and paper pieces. Repeat to stitch six red and six green medium petals together to make a medium Dresden flower. Stitch eight red and eight green large petals together to make a large Dresden flower.

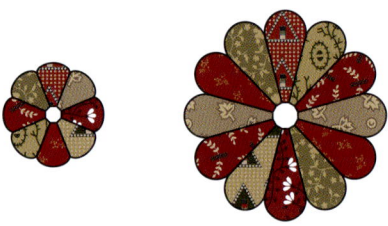

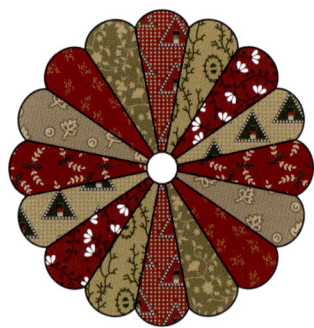

Make 1 of each.

3. Alternating the four red and three green ¾" hexagons, whipstitch them together for the vase band. Press well; remove basting and paper pieces.

4. Center the stems, Dresden flowers, hexagon flower centers, vase, and handles onto the pieced background rectangle and appliqué in place, spacing the Dresden flowers 1⅜" apart and placing the vase 1" up from the bottom edge. Lay the hexagon band on top of the vase, 2½" down from the vase's top edge.

Open up the seam allowance on the outer edge of the end hexagons and then fold over the hexagons to align with the side edges of the vase and press. Appliqué in place by hand or machine.

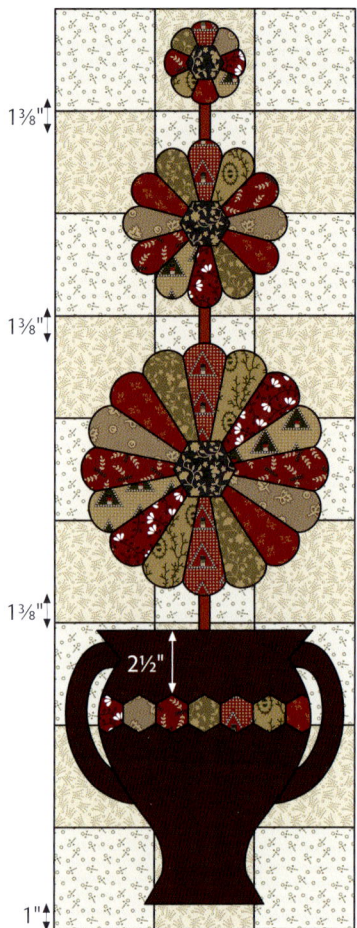

Assembling the Quilt Top

1. With right sides together, stitch the 1½" x 12½" black strips to the top and bottom of the wall hanging. Press seam allowances toward the black strips. Stitch a 1½" x 38½" black strip to each side. Press.

2. Stitch the 3½" x 14½" floral strips to the top and bottom of the wall hanging. Press seam allowances toward the outer border. Stitch a 3½" black square to each end of the 3½" x 38½" floral strips, pressing

seam allowances toward the floral strips. Stitch one of these border strips to each side of the wall hanging. Press seam allowances toward the outer border.

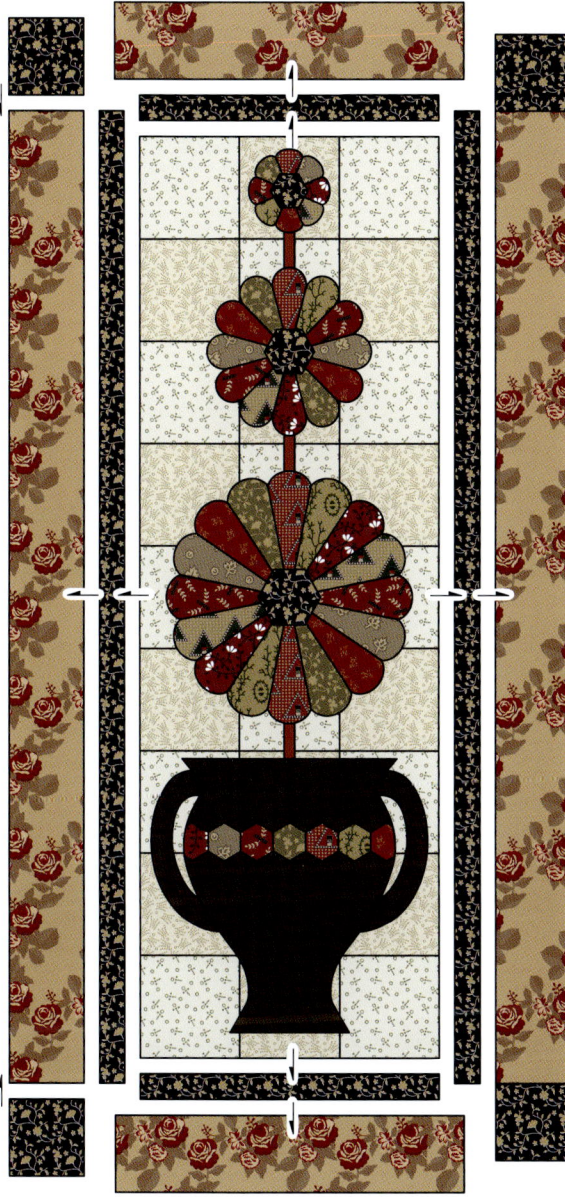

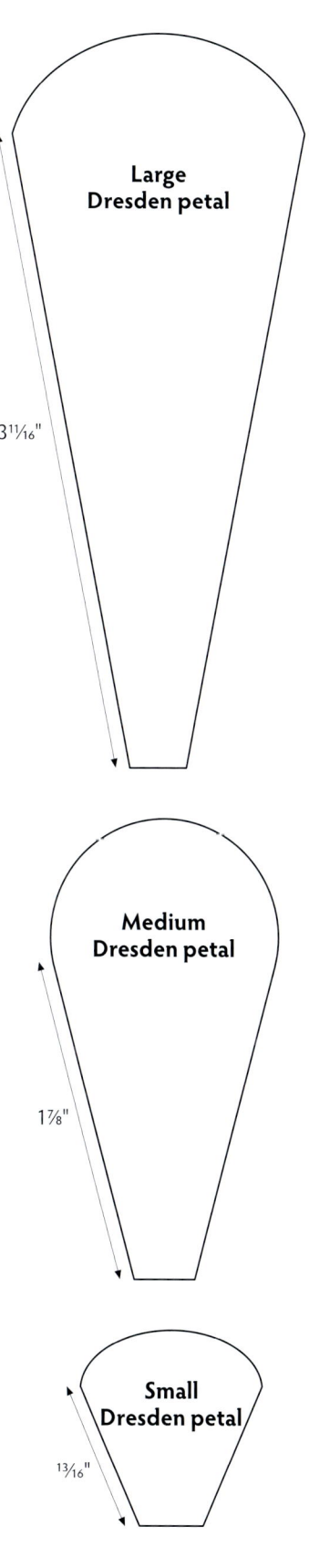

Large Dresden petal

3 11/16"

Medium Dresden petal

1 7/8"

Small Dresden petal

13/16"

Patterns do not include seam allowances.

Finishing

Refer to page 12 or details on marking, layering, basting, and quilting your project. Then use the 2"-wide black-print strips to bind the wall hanging.

Topiary

Vase

Join to pattern on page 19 along dashed line to complete pattern.

Pattern does not include seam allowances.

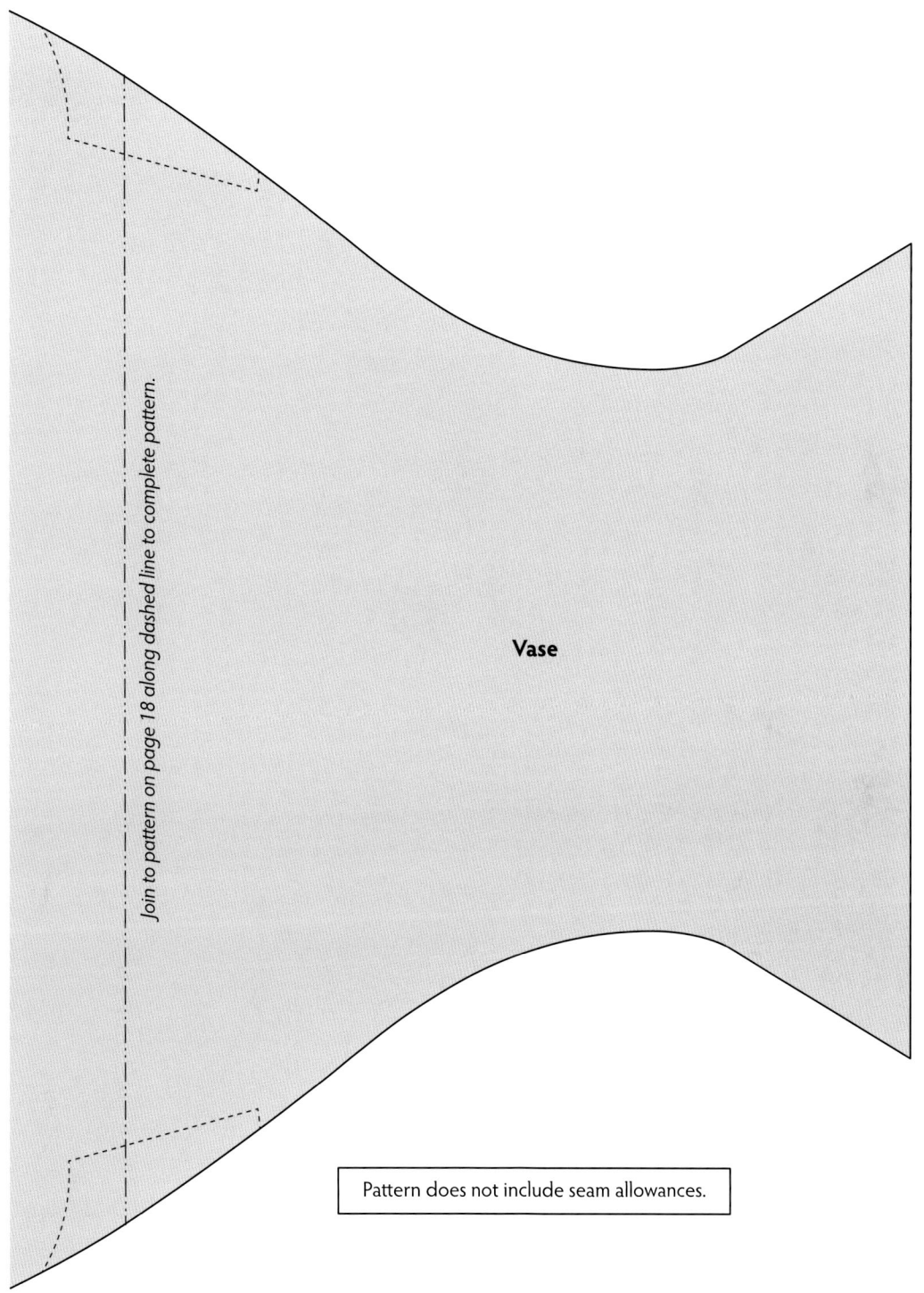

Stem
Make 3.

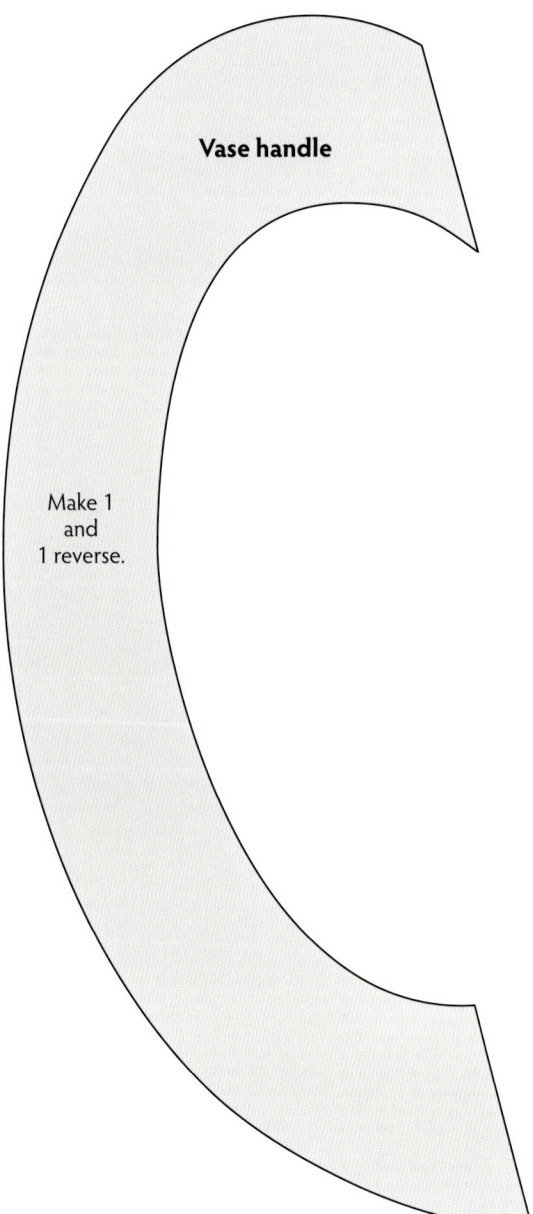

Vase handle

Make 1
and
1 reverse.

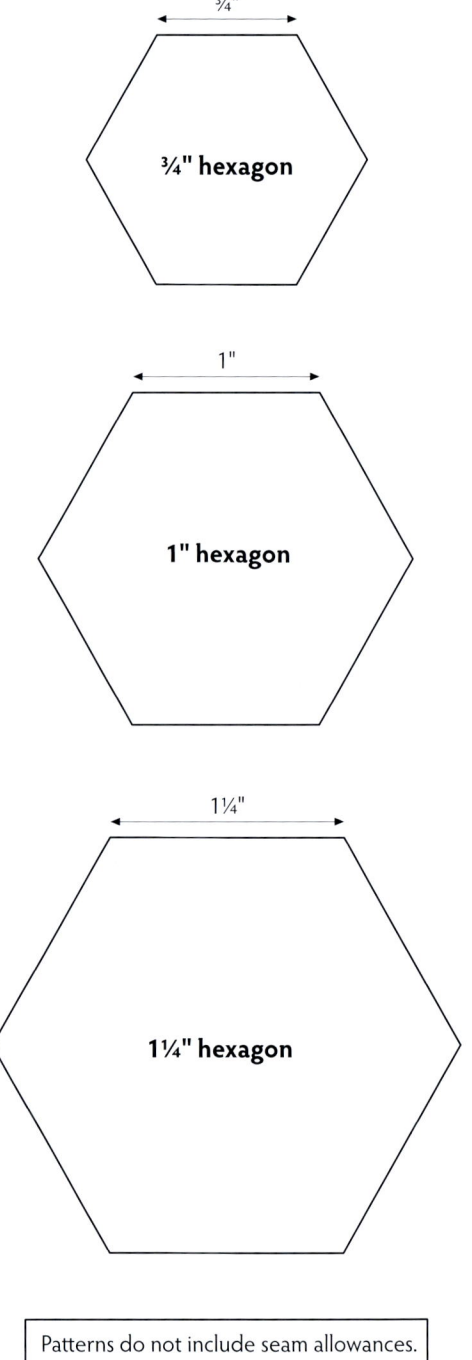

¾"

¾" hexagon

1"

1" hexagon

1¼"

1¼" hexagon

Patterns do not include seam allowances.

Simple Splendor

There is something so dramatic and appealing about Dresden plates! With all of the shapes and sizes that are now available at paperpieces.com, they have become one of my favorites. I'm not sure if it's because they remind me of beautiful antique quilts that I often see at quilt shows, or because of the way they "pop" in a quilt. Often a simple quilt design is the perfect way to showcase Dresden plates.

FINISHED QUILT: 48½" x 48½"

Materials

Yardage is based on 42"-wide fabric.
1⅝ yards of light print #1 for background
1⅓ yards of light print #2 for background
⅝ yard of black print for flower centers and binding
1 fat quarter *each* of 2 reds, 2 blues, and 2 greens for pieced blocks and appliqués
1 fat eighth *each* of 2 golds and 2 browns for pieced blocks and appliqués
3 yards of fabric for backing
53" x 53" piece of batting
16 large Dresden blade papers, 3¹¹⁄₁₆"
40 medium Dresden blade papers, 2⅜"
40 small Dresden blade papers, 2"
56 leaf papers, 2¾"
1 large circle paper, 2"
4 medium circle papers, 1⅝"
4 small circle papers, 1⅛"
Size 7, 8, or 9 Sharp needle and thread to match fabric
Appliqué glue and freezer paper **OR** ¼ yard of lightweight fusible web, 18" wide

Cutting

Refer to "English Paper Piecing" on page 5 for cutting Dresden blades, leaves, and circles; baste all shapes to the papers. Refer to "Quiltmaking Basics" on page 9 to prepare the stems for appliqué. Patterns are on page 25.

From *each* of the 2 red prints, cut:
1 rectangle, 4½" x 8½"
2 squares, 4½" x 4½"
2 large, 4 medium, and 4 small Dresden blades
4 leaves

From *each* of the 2 blue prints, cut:
1 rectangle, 4½" x 8½"
2 squares, 4½" x 4½"
2 large, 4 medium, and 4 small Dresden blades

From *each* of the 2 green prints, cut:
2 squares, 4½" x 4½"
2 large, 4 medium, and 4 small Dresden blades
4 stems
16 leaves

From *each* of the 2 brown prints, cut:
2 squares, 4½" x 4½"
1 large, 4 medium, and 4 small Dresden blades
4 leaves

From *each* of the 2 gold prints, cut:
4 squares, 4½" x 4½"
1 large, 4 medium, and 4 small Dresden blades
4 leaves

From light print #1, cut:
2 strips, 8½" x 42"; crosscut into 5 squares, 8½" x 8½", and 8 rectangles, 4½" x 8½"
6 strips, 4½" x 42"; crosscut 2 of the strips into 10 squares, 4½" x 4½"

From light print #2, cut:
4 squares, 8½" x 8½"
7 strips, 4½" x 42"; crosscut 3 of the strips into 4 rectangles, 4½" x 8½", and 10 squares, 4½" x 4½"

From the black print, cut:
1 large, 4 medium, and 4 small circles
6 strips, 2" x 42"

Making the Dresden Blocks

1. Whipstitch the 16 assorted large Dresden blades together to make one large Dresden plate. Set aside until quilt assembly.

Make 1.

2. Whipstitch 10 assorted small Dresden blades together (two each of brown, red, blue, green, and gold). Make four small Dresden plates and set aside for appliquéing the borders.

Make 4.

3. Whipstitch 10 assorted medium Dresden blades together (two each of brown, red, blue, green, and gold). Make four medium Dresden plates. Press well on both sides and remove basting and paper pieces.

Make 4.

4. Center a medium Dresden plate onto an 8½" light-print square and hand or machine appliqué in place. Center a black medium circle onto the Dresden plate and appliqué in place. Make four, two with each of the light-print backgrounds.

Making the Flying Geese

1. Draw a diagonal line from corner to corner on the wrong side of all of the 4½" brown, green, blue, red, and gold squares. Repeat for four 4½" squares each of the two light prints.

2. With right sides together, lay a 4½" brown-print square onto a 4½" x 8½" light-print #1 rectangle. Stitch on the drawn line, trim, and press toward the brown. Repeat with a 4½" green-print square on the opposite end as shown. Make two of these flying-geese units. Repeat with the squares of the second brown print and second green print to make two flying-geese units.

Make 2 of each.

3. Repeat step 2 to make 12 additional flying-geese units with the fabrics shown.

Make 2 of each.   Make 2 of each.

Make 1 of each.   Make 1 of each.

Assembling the Quilt Top

1. Sew a red-and-gold flying-geese unit to a medium Dresden block as shown. Sew a blue-and-gold flying-geese unit to a 4½" light square. Join the two units. Make four, two with each of the light prints.

2. Arrange a blue flying-geese unit, a brown-and-green flying-geese unit, and two 4½" light squares as shown. Sew together in rows and then sew the rows together. Make two. Repeat to make two using the red flying-geese units.

 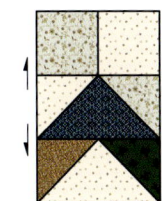 

Make 2 of each.

Simple Splendor

3. Arrange the units from steps 1 and 2 together with an 8½" square of light print #1 as shown. Sew together in rows and then sew the rows together.

4. Center the large Dresden plate and large black circle in place in the center of the unit from step 3 and hand or machine appliqué to the quilt.

Adding the Border

1. With right sides together, stitch each 4½"-wide light-print #1 strip to a 4½"-wide light-print #2 strip. Make four strip sets. Crosscut the strip sets at 4½" intervals to make a total of 32 two-patch segments measuring 4½" x 8½".

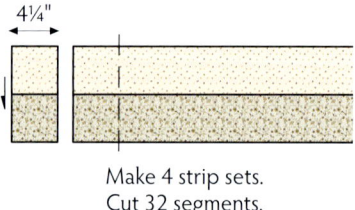

Make 4 strip sets.
Cut 32 segments.

2. Stitch eight of the strip-set segments together to make a border measuring 8½" x 32½", noting the orientation of the two-patch units. Make two of each orientation as shown.

Make 2.

Make 2.

3. Center a small Dresden plate, a small circle, two stems, and 14 leaves (eight green, two red, two gold, and two brown) onto each border and appliqué in place.

4. Stitch appliquéd borders to the top and bottom of the quilt, pressing seam allowances toward the border strips.

5. Stitch an 8½" light-print #1 square to one end of each remaining border strip. Stitch an 8½" light-print #2 square to the opposite end. Press the seam allowances toward the appliquéd border. Stitch one of these borders to each side of the quilt. Press the seam allowances toward the appliquéd border.

Quilt assembly

Finishing

Refer to page 12 for details on marking, layering, basting, and quilting your project. Then use the 2"-wide black print strips to bind the quilt.

English Paper Piecing II

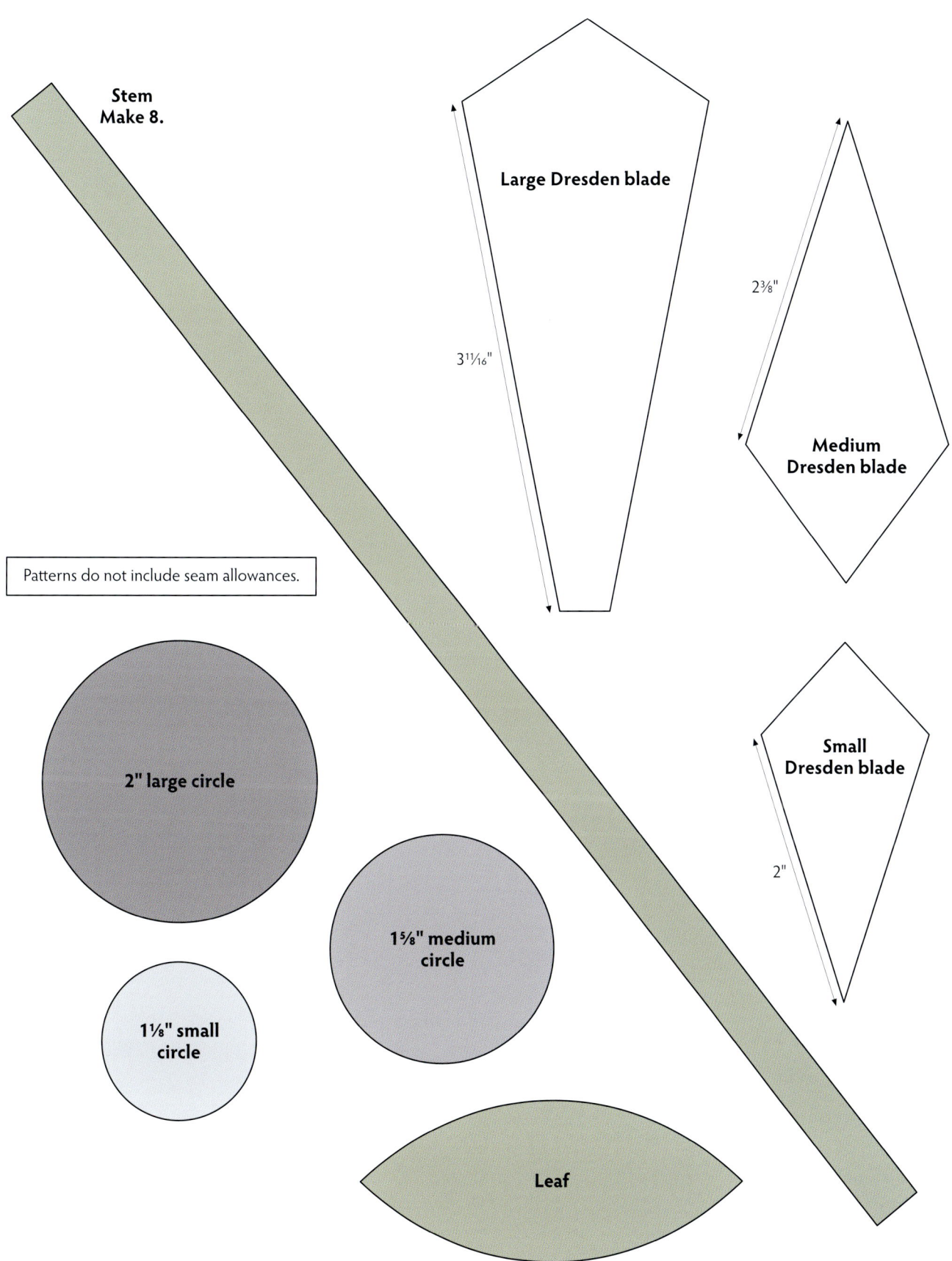

Cover-Up Duo

After redecorating my quilting studio, I really wanted sewing-machine covers to coordinate with my new color scheme. I knew these would be next to impossible to find ready made, so I designed two different styles and sizes that will accommodate a wide variety of sewing machines.

Small/Medium Cover-Up

Instructions for the medium/large cover start on page 30.

FINISHED SIZE: 9½" x 15½" x 6"

Materials

Yardage is based on 42"-wide fabric.

1 fat quarter of large-scale red-and-cream print for cover front and gusset
1 fat quarter of light print for octagons, squares, and cover back
1 fat eighth *each* of 3 assorted red prints for octagons, squares, and binding
1 fat eighth *each* of 3 assorted gray prints for octagons, squares, and binding
⅝ yard of fabric for lining
⅝ yard of fusible fleece, such as Thermolam*
84 octagon papers, ½"
65 square papers, ½"
Size 7, 8, or 9 Sharp needle and thread to match fabric

*Fusible fleece is stiffer than regular batting and gives the cover extra body.

Cutting

Refer to "English Paper Piecing" on page 5 for cutting octagons and squares; baste all shapes to the papers. Patterns are on page 29.

From *each* of the 3 assorted red and 3 assorted gray prints, cut:
2 rectangles, 2½" x 4½"
8 octagons
2 squares

From the light print, cut:
1 strip, 9½" x 16"
36 octagons
53 squares

From the red-and-cream print, cut:
2 strips, 6½" x 16¾"
1 strip, 3½" x 16"

From the fusible fleece, cut:
2 rectangles, 9½" x 16"
1 strip, 6½" x 33"

From the lining fabric, cut:
1 strip, 9½" x 42"; crosscut into 2 rectangles, 9½" x 16"
1 strip, 6½" x 33"

> **TIP FOR TINY SQUARES**
> Use a small dab of glue from a glue pen in the center of each square to keep it in place on the fabric when cutting and basting.

Making the Octagon Flowers

1. Whipstitch four matching red-print octagons to a gray-print square. Make six octagon flowers with the assorted red prints. Whipstitch four matching gray-print octagons to a red-print square. Make six.

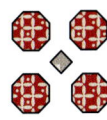

Make 6 of each.

2. Alternating gray and red octagon flowers and light-print squares, whipstitch together two rows of flowers. Press well; remove the basting and paper pieces from the interior squares and octagons.

3. Whipstitch the remaining light-print octagons and squares to the unit from step 2. Press well on both sides and remove all remaining basting and paper pieces.

4. Draw cutting lines on all four sides of the octagon unit to measure 6½" x 16". Stitch a scant ⅛" inside of the drawn lines to reinforce the whipstitching before trimming. Using a rotary cutter, trim all four sides on the drawn lines to make the cover front.

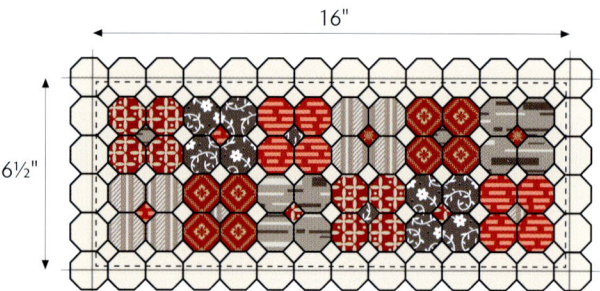

5. With right sides together, stitch the 3½" x 16" red-and-cream strip to the top of the cover front. Press seam allowances toward the strip.

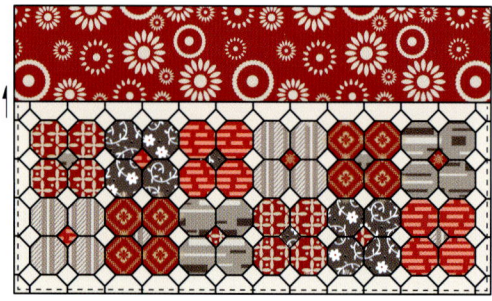

6. Fuse a 9½" x 16" piece of Thermolam to the wrong side of the cover front, and fuse the second 9½" x 16" piece of Thermolam to the wrong side of the 9½" x 16" light-print rectangle for the cover back.

7. With wrong sides together, baste a 9½" x 16" lining piece to the cover front around all four sides using a scant ¼" seam allowance. Repeat to baste the second 9½" x 16" lining piece to the cover back.

8. Trace the corner curve pattern on page 29 onto paper. Mark the curve on the right side of the top corners of the cover front and back. Trim on the drawn lines through all layers.

9. With right sides together, stitch the 6½" x 16¾" red-and-cream strips together end to end to make a gusset measuring 33". Fuse the 6½" x 33" piece of Thermolam to the wrong side of the gusset. With wrong sides together, baste the 6½" x 33" lining strip to the gusset on all four sides using a scant ¼" seam allowance.

Assembling the Cover

1. With right sides together, pin and stitch the gusset to the sides and top of the cover front, easing in fullness around the corners. Repeat to stitch the remaining side of the gusset to the cover back.

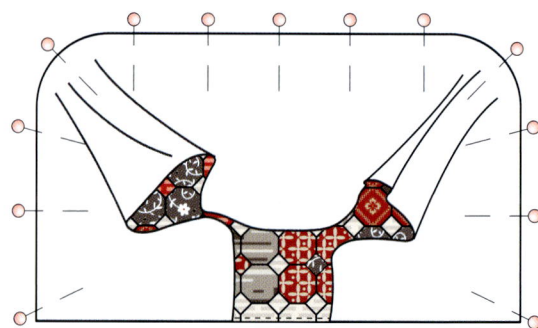

2. Serge or zigzag stitch the raw edges of the gusset seam allowance and turn right side out.

Finishing

Stitch the assorted 2½" x 4½" red- and gray-print rectangles together end to end, pressing the seam allowances open. Use this 48½"-long strip to bind the bottom edge of the cover.

English Paper Piecing II

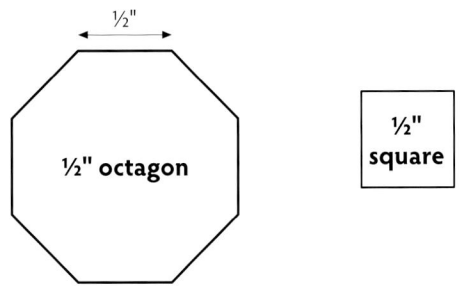

½"

½" octagon

½" square

Patterns do not include seam allowances.

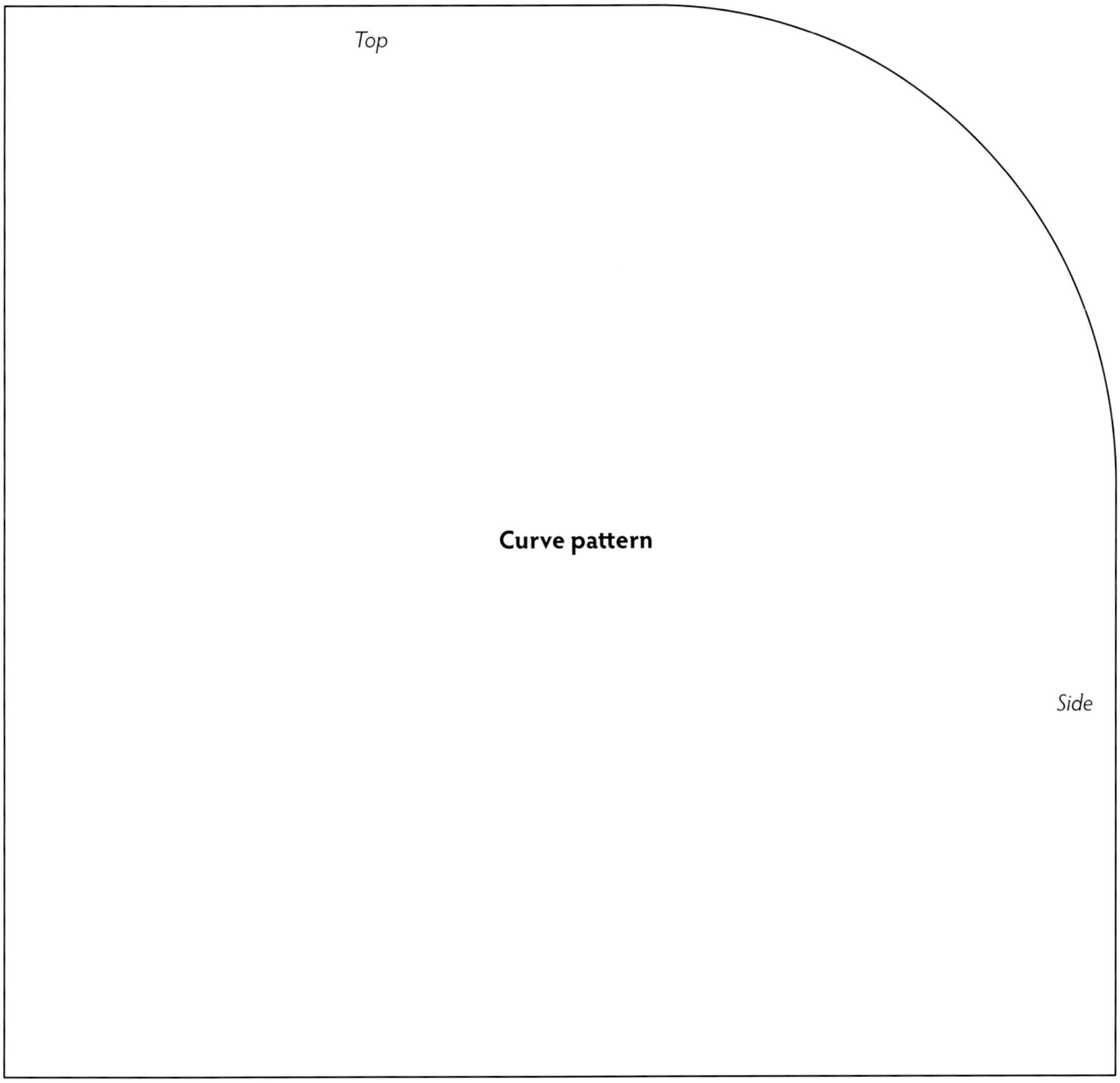

Top

Curve pattern

Side

Cover-Up Duo

Medium/Large Cover-Up

FINISHED SIZE: 12½" x 18¼" x 6½"

Materials

Yardage is based on 42"-wide fabric.

1 fat quarter of small-scale gray polka dot for cover front, back, and leaves
1 fat quarter of light print for front appliqué background
1 fat quarter of large-scale red polka dot for gusset*
1 fat quarter of dark-gray fabric for squares, stems, and binding
Scraps of red print #1 and red print #2 for octagons (10" square or 2½" x 18" strip of each)
¾ yard of fabric for lining
20 octagon papers, ¾"
5 square papers, ¾"
10 leaf papers, 2"
⅔ yard of fusible fleece such as Thermolam**
Size 7, 8, or 9 Sharp needle and thread to match fabric
Appliqué glue and freezer paper **OR** ¼ yard of lightweight fusible web, 18" wide

*The fat quarter should measure at least 21½" wide after removing the selvage. If it doesn't, you'll need a ½-yard cut of fabric.

**Fusible fleece is stiffer than regular batting and gives the cover extra body.

Cutting

Refer to "English Paper Piecing" on page 5 for cutting octagons and squares; baste all shapes to the papers. Refer to "Quiltmaking Basics" on page 9 to prepare the stems and leaves for appliqué. Patterns are on pages 29 and 32.

From red print #1, cut:
12 octagons

From the dark-gray fabric, cut:
3 strips, 2½" x 22"
3 long stems
2 short stems
5 squares

From red print #2, cut:
8 octagons

From the gray polka dot, cut:
1 rectangle, 12½" x 18¾"
1 strip, 2½" x 18¾"
10 leaves

From the light print, cut:
1 rectangle, 10½" x 18¾"

From the fusible fleece, cut:
2 rectangles, 12½" x 18¾"
1 strip, 7" x 41¾"

From the lining fabric, cut:
2 rectangles, 12½" x 18¾"
1 strip, 7" x 41¾"

From the red polka dot, cut:
2 strips, 7" x 21⅛"

Making the Octagon Flowers

1. Whipstitch four octagons of red print #1 to a gray square to make an octagon flower. Make three octagon flowers using red print #1 and two using red print #2.

  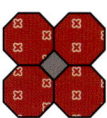

Make 3. Make 2.

2. Whipstitch the octagon flowers together as shown. Press well on both sides; remove basting and paper pieces.

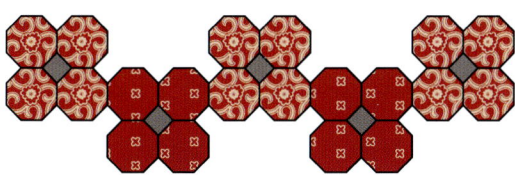

3. Position the octagon flower strip, two short stems, three long stems, and 10 leaves onto the 10½" x 18¾" light-print rectangle, referring to the step 4 diagram for placement. Apply a few drops of appliqué glue near the outer edges on the wrong side of each piece and finger-press in place. Appliqué to the light-print rectangle by hand or machine.

4. With right sides together, stitch the 2½" x 18¾" gray polka-dot strip to the flower unit, pressing the seam allowances toward the gray strip.

5. Fuse a 12½" x 18¾" piece of Thermolam to the wrong side of the cover front, and fuse the second 12½" x 18¾" piece of Thermolam to the wrong side of the 12½" x 18¾" gray polka-dot rectangle for the cover back.

6. With wrong sides together, baste a 12½" x 18¾" lining piece to the cover front around all four sides using a scant ¼" seam allowance. Repeat to baste the second 12½" x 18¾" lining piece to the cover back.

7. Trace the curve pattern on page 29 onto paper. Mark the curve on the right side of the top corners of the cover front and back. Trim on the drawn lines through all layers.

8. With right sides together, stitch the 7" x 21⅛" red polka-dot strips together for a gusset measuring 41¾". Fuse the 7" x 41¾" piece of Thermolam to the wrong side of the gusset. With wrong sides together, baste the 7" x 41¾" lining strip to the gusset on all four sides using a scant ¼" seam allowance.

Assembling and Finishing

Referring to page 28 of the small/medium project, repeat the instructions in "Assembling the Cover" and "Finishing" to complete the cover-up and bind it with the 2½"-wide gray strips.

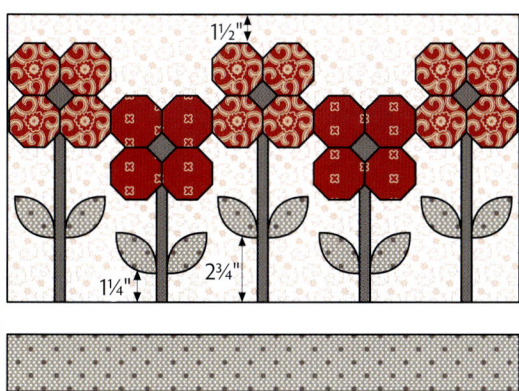

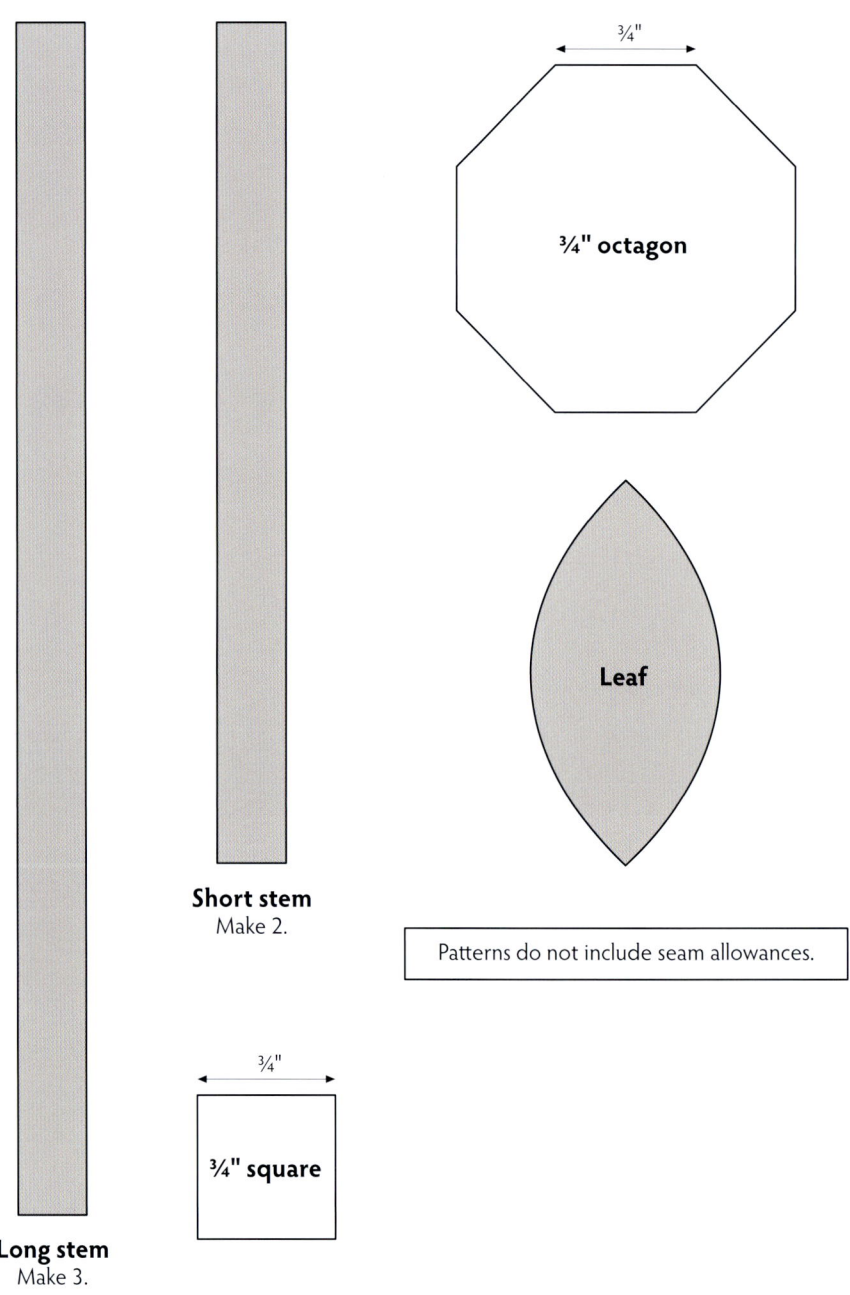

Long stem
Make 3.

Short stem
Make 2.

¾"

¾" octagon

Leaf

Patterns do not include seam allowances.

¾"

¾" square

Little Dresden Patch

There's something so adorable about miniature projects, and I have the perfect spot in my house for this one. Dainty Dresdens and a scalloped border make this a charming table topper or wall hanging. I chose patriotic colors, but made in feminine pastels, this would be a wonderful addition to a little girl's room.

FINISHED QUILT: 23" x 23"
FINISHED BLOCK: 4½" x 4½"

Materials

Yardage is based on 42"-wide fabric.

½ yard of red print #1 for hexagons, inner border, and binding

⅓ yard of light-tan print for sashing and outer border

1 fat quarter of light print for block backgrounds

1 fat eighth *each* of 6 assorted small-scale blue prints for flowers and border scallops

1 fat eighth of red print #2 for hexagons, sashing squares, and border corner squares

⅞ yard of fabric for backing

27" x 27" piece of batting

54 Dresden petal papers*, ¾"

9 hexagon papers, ¾"

36 scallop papers, 2"

Size 7, 8, or 9 Sharp needle and thread to match fabric

Appliqué glue

*These are referred to as Hex Den petals on paperpieces.com.

Cutting

Refer to "English Paper Piecing" on page 5 for cutting Dresden petals, hexagons, and scallops; baste all shapes to the papers. Patterns are on page 35.

From *each* of the 6 assorted blue prints, cut:
9 Dresden petals
6 scallops

From the red print #2, cut:
4 squares, 2¾" x 2¾"
4 squares, 1½" x 1½"
5 hexagons

From the red print #1, cut:
2 strips, 1¾" x 42"; crosscut into 2 strips, 1¾" x 16", and 2 strips, 1¾" x 18½"
4 hexagons
3 strips, 2" x 42"

From the light print, cut:
9 squares, 5" x 5"

From the light-tan print, cut:
2 strips, 2¾" x 42"; crosscut into 4 strips, 2¾" x 18½"
2 strips, 1½" x 42"; crosscut into 12 rectangles, 1½" x 5"

Making the Dresden Flower Blocks

1. Whipstitch six Dresden petals, one of each blue print, to a red hexagon to make a flower. Make five flowers with a red-print #2 hexagon and four flowers with a red-print #1 hexagon. Press well on both sides, and remove the basting and paper pieces.

2. Fold each 5" light-print square in half in both directions and finger-press to create a placement guide. Using the creases, center a Dresden flower onto each square and hand or machine appliqué in place.

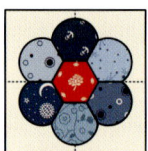

Make 9.

Assembling the Quilt Top

1. Arrange the flower blocks in three rows of three blocks each, alternating the two different red hexagons. Add the 1½" x 5" light-tan rectangles between the blocks in each row and between the rows, adding the 1½" red-print #2 sashing squares. Sew the blocks and sashing rectangles into rows. Sew the sashing rectangles and sashing squares into rows. Press as shown. Join the rows and press toward the sashing rows. The quilt center should now measure 16" x 16".

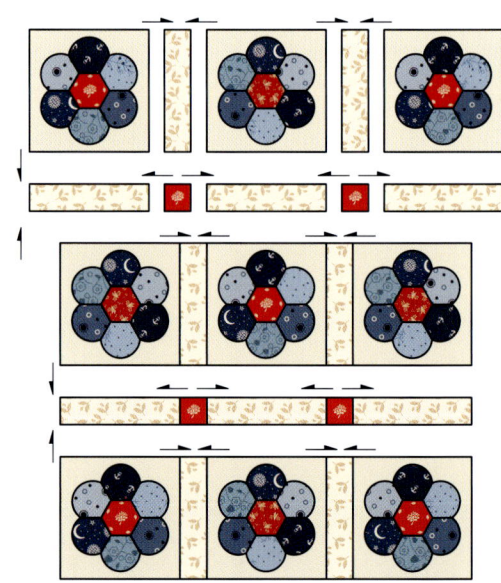

2. Stitch the 1¾" x 16" red-print #1 strips to the top and bottom of the quilt center. Press seam allowances toward the strips. Stitch a 1¾" x 18½" red-print #1 strip to each side and press.

3. Alternating the prints, whipstitch together nine blue scallops. Begin stitching at the bottom straight edge and stitch upward approximately 1". Make four scallop strips. Press well on both sides; remove basting and paper pieces.

4. Center a scallop strip onto each of the 2¾" x 18½" light-tan strips, aligning the straight edges. Hand or machine appliqué in place along the scalloped edge.

5. With right sides together, stitch the scalloped borders to the top and bottom of the quilt. Press seam allowances toward the red inner border. Stitch a 2¾" red-print #2 square to each end of the remaining two scalloped borders and press toward the red squares. Stitch a border strip to each side of the quilt; press.

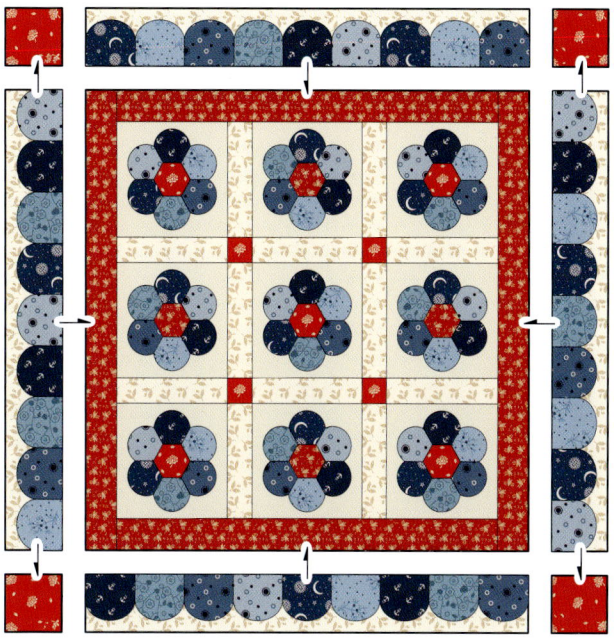

Finishing

Refer to page 12 for details on marking, layering, basting, and quilting your project. Then use the 2"-wide red-print strips to bind the quilt.

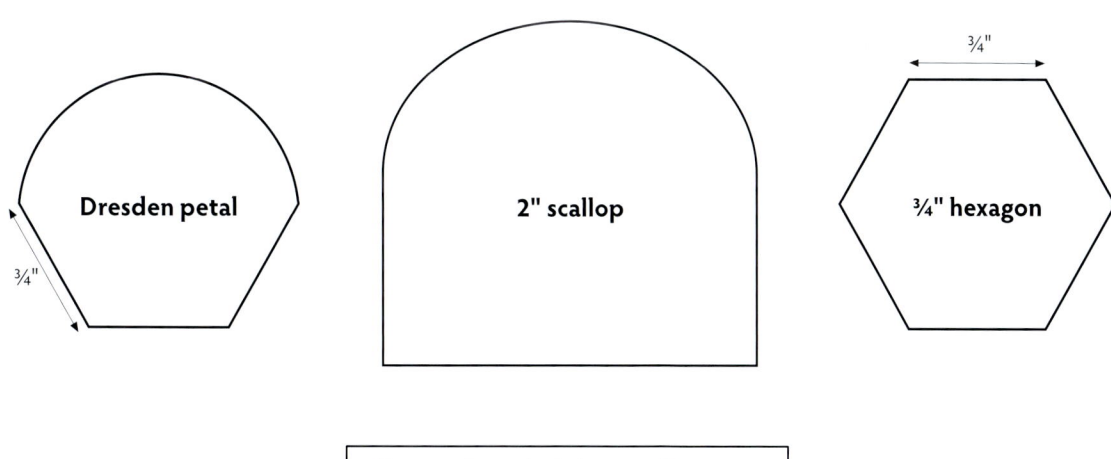

Patterns do not include seam allowances.

Little Dresden Patch 35

In Full Bloom

Every year as soon as the weather turns warm and sunny, my husband and I like to spend a weekend planting flowers in our courtyard. We have numerous large pots, as well as flower beds, so it takes quite a bit of planning, shopping at the nursery, and then "down and dirty" work to plant it all. The effort is always worth it as soon as everything starts to bloom, and we usually have a few months to enjoy the period of "full bloom," which is always one of my favorite times of the year.

FINISHED QUILT: 46" x 46"

Materials

Yardage is based on 42"-wide fabric.

1⅓ yards of large-scale floral for sashing, blocks, and border
1⅓ yards of light print for blocks and border corners
½ yard of red tone on tone for sashing cornerposts and binding
¼ yard of green tone on tone for leaves and stems
1 fat eighth *each* of blue, red, green, and gold prints for flowers
3 yards of fabric for backing
50" x 50" piece of batting
72 Dresden petal papers, 1¹¹⁄₁₆"
9 circle papers, 2"
Size 7, 8, or 9 Sharp needle and thread to match fabric
Appliqué glue and freezer paper **OR** ½ yard of lightweight fusible web, 18" wide

Cutting

Refer to "English Paper Piecing" on page 5 for cutting Dresden petals and circles; baste all shapes to the papers. Refer to "Quiltmaking Basics" on page 9 to prepare the leaves and stems for appliqué. Patterns are on page 39.

From *each* of the blue, red, green, and gold prints, cut:
18 Dresden petals

From the green tone on tone, cut:
16 leaves
4 long stems
4 short stems

From the light print, cut:
3 strips, 12½" x 42"; crosscut into:
  4 rectangles, 8½" x 12½"
  4 squares, 12½" x 12½"
  1 square, 8½" x 8½"
  2 squares, 7" x 7"
9 circles

From the floral, cut:
4 strips, 6½" x 42"; crosscut into 4 strips, 6½" x 34½"
1 strip, 7" x 42"; crosscut into 2 squares, 7" x 7", and 4 squares, 6½" x 6½"
4 strips, 1½" x 42"; crosscut into 8 rectangles, 1½" x 12½", and 4 rectangles, 1½" x 8½"

From the red tone on tone, cut:
4 squares, 1½" x 1½"
5 strips, 2" x 42"

Making the Flower Blocks

1. Whipstitch eight Dresden petals together (two each of blue, red, green, and gold) to make a flower. Press well on both sides; remove the basting and paper pieces. Make nine.

Make 9.

2. Place one flower, one circle, two leaves, and one short stem onto each of the light-print 8½" x 12½" rectangles as shown. Hand or machine appliqué in place.

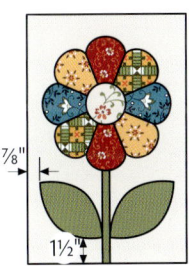

Make 4.

3. Draw a diagonal line from corner to corner on the wrong side of each 6½" floral square. With right sides together, lay a marked square on the corner of a light-print 12½" square. Stitch on the drawn line, trim, and press the seam allowances toward the floral triangle.

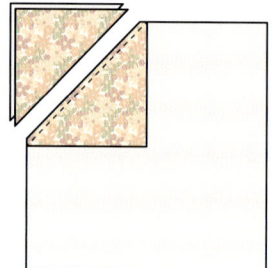 

Make 4.

4. Place one flower, one circle, two leaves, and one long stem onto each of the blocks from step 3 as shown, placing the stem on the diagonal. Hand or machine appliqué in place.

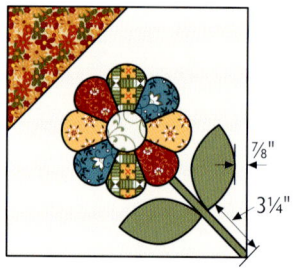

Make 4.

5. Fold the 8½" light-print square in half in both directions and crease to mark the center. Center the remaining Dresden flower and circle onto the square and appliqué in place by hand or machine.

Assembling the Quilt Top

1. Arrange the blocks, sashing strips, and sashing cornerposts in rows as shown. Sew the pieces in each row together and press the seam allowances toward the sashing. Sew the rows together and press the seam allowances toward the sashing rows.

2. Stitch 6½" x 34½" floral strips to the top and bottom of the quilt and press the seam allowances toward the border.

3. Draw a diagonal line from corner to corner on the wrong side of each 7" light-print square. With right sides together, layer a marked square on a 7" floral square. Stitch ¼" from the drawn line on each side. Cut on the drawn line and press the seam allowances toward the floral. Trim and square up to 6½" x 6½". Make four half-square-triangle units.

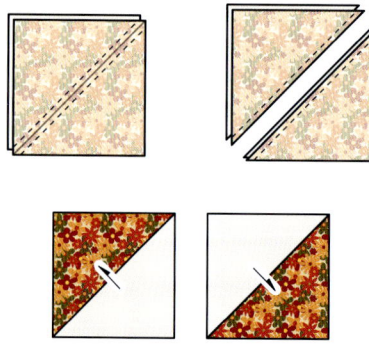

Make 4.

English Paper Piecing II

4. Stitch a half-square-triangle unit to each end of the remaining 6½" x 34½" floral strips, pressing the seam allowances toward the strips. Stitch one of these borders to each side of the quilt and press.

Finishing

Refer to page 12 for details on marking, layering, basting, and quilting your project. Then use the 2"-wide red tone-on-tone strips to bind the quilt.

Short stem
Make 4.

Long stem
Make 4.

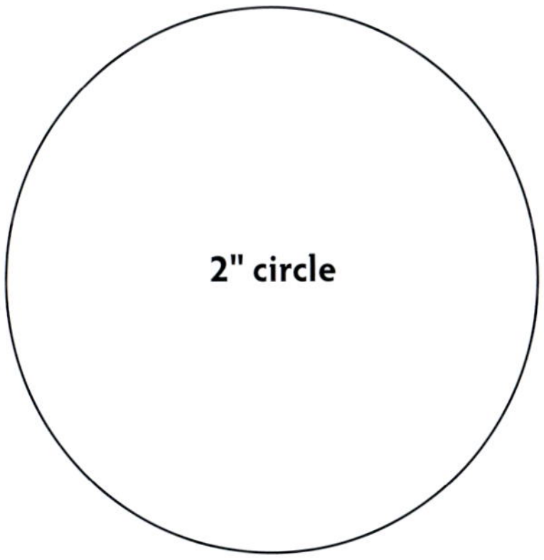

2" circle

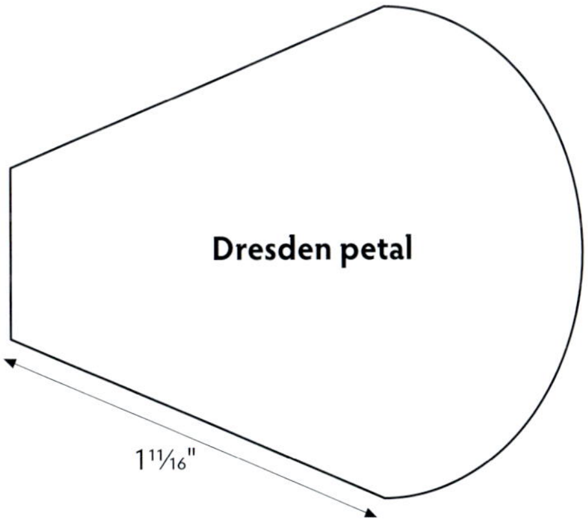

Dresden petal

1¹¹⁄₁₆"

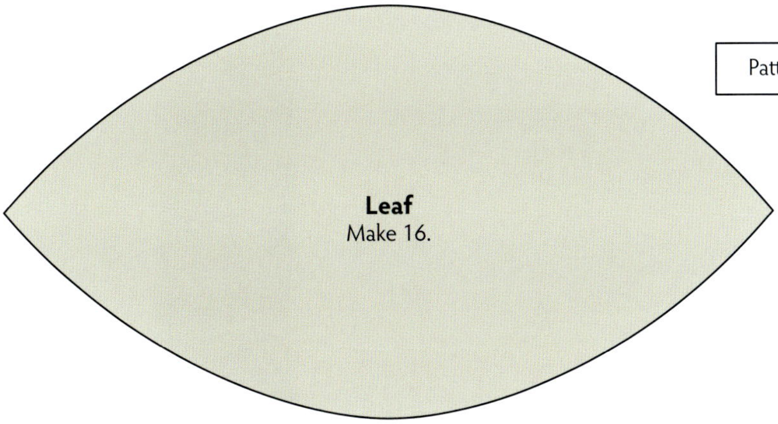

Leaf
Make 16.

Patterns do not include seam allowances.

In Full Bloom 39

Fig Tree Flowers

I'm the first to admit that I enjoy instant-gratification projects! However, I always like to have one English-paper-piecing project that I can work on for several months, especially one that allows me to dip into my stash for the fabrics I need. Here I used by collection of Fig Tree fabrics. I call this my "go-to" project, something I know I can work on every evening while I am watching television or while traveling.

FINISHED QUILT: 60" x 77½"

Materials

Yardage is based on 42"-wide fabric.

3 yards of yellow print or tone on tone for hexagons and binding

3 yards *total* of assorted medium to dark prints for hexagon flowers

2½ yards *total* of assorted light prints for hexagon flowers

2¼ yards of peach check for border

⅜ yard *total* of assorted green prints for leaves (at least 2½" x 2½" squares)

⅓ yard of green solid for stems and leaves

4¾ yards of fabric for backing

66" x 84" piece of batting

2,031 hexagon papers, ¾"

42 half hexagon papers, ¾"

76 leaf papers*, 2"

Size 7, 8, or 9 Sharp needle and thread to match fabric

Appliqué glue and freezer paper **OR** ¾ yard of lightweight fusible web, 18" wide

*These are referred to as Flower Petals on paperpieces.com.

Cutting

Refer to "English Paper Piecing" on page 5 for cutting hexagons, half hexagons, and leaves; baste all shapes to the papers. Baste half hexagons leaving the long straight edge raw and even with the paper. Refer to "Quiltmaking Basics" on page 9 to prepare the stems for appliqué. Patterns are on page 45.

From the assorted medium to dark prints, cut:
132 matching sets of 6 hexagons

From the yellow, cut:
583 squares, 2⅛" x 2⅛" (for hexagons)
42 half hexagons
8 strips, 2" x 42"

From the assorted light prints, cut:
99 matching sets of 6 hexagons
22 matching pairs of hexagons
18 hexagons

From the peach check, cut on the *lengthwise* grain:
2 strips, 7½" x 48"*
2 strips, 7½" x 78"*

From the green solid, cut:
12 stems

From the assorted green prints, cut a total of:
76 leaves

*Border strips are cut longer than needed; be sure to measure your quilt before cutting and adding borders.

Making the Hexagon Flowers

1. Whipstitch six matching medium or dark hexagons together with one yellow hexagon center to make a flower. Repeat to make 132 medium to dark hexagon flowers.

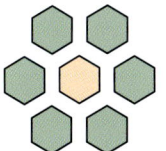
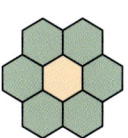

Make 132.

2. Repeat step 1 using six matching light hexagons and one yellow hexagon. Make 99 light hexagon flowers.

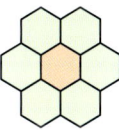

Make 99.

3. Whipstitch together the 22 pairs of matching light hexagons. Set aside the remaining 18 light hexagons.

Make 22.

Fig Tree Flowers

Assembling the Quilt Top

1. Whipstitch 10 medium to dark hexagon flowers and nine yellow hexagons together as shown to make row 1. For row 2, whipstitch together nine light hexagon flowers, 10 yellow hexagons, and two pairs of light hexagons. Make 12 of row 1 and 11 of row 2.

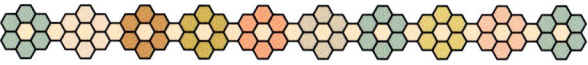

Row 1. Make 12.

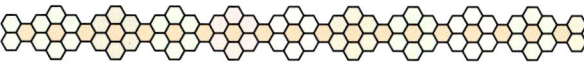

Row 2. Make 11.

2. Whipstitch row 1 to row 2.

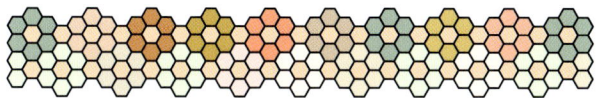

3. Continue alternating rows 1 and 2 until you have whipstitched together 23 rows. You'll end with a medium to dark row 1. As you sew, you can remove the papers from hexagons that are no longer on an outside edge.

4. Whipstitch 47 yellow hexagons to both the right and left sides of the quilt center. Whipstitch nine light hexagons and 21 yellow half hexagons to both the top and bottom of the quilt center.

5. Press the quilt well on both sides. Remove basting and paper pieces from all hexagons.

TAME THE EDGES
Before pressing and removing the paper pieces, spray around the outside yellow edges with sizing. This will give you edges that are smooth and flat.

6. Draw cutting lines on the right and left sides of the quilt as shown. Stay stitch along each side just inside of the drawn line to prevent any whipstitching from coming apart when the hexagons are cut off. After stay stitching, press the outside yellow hexagons again to ensure they are nice and flat, and then cut each side on the drawn line.

Adding the Border

1. Measure the width of your quilt through the center and cut the 7½" x 48" peach strips to that length for the top and bottom borders.

2. Center two stems, three flowers, and 12 leaves in place on the peach strips. Hand or machine appliqué in place.

3. Stitch the appliquéd border strips to the top and bottom of the quilt, pressing seam allowances toward the border.

4. Measure the length of your quilt through the center, including the borders just added, and cut the 7½" x 78" peach strips to that length for the side borders.

5. Center four stems, three flowers, and 26 leaves on each border strip. Appliqué in place by hand or machine.

6. Stitch the side borders to the quilt. Press seam allowances toward the border.

Finishing

Refer to page 12 for details on marking, layering, basting, and quilting your project. Then use the 2"-wide yellow strips to bind the quilt.

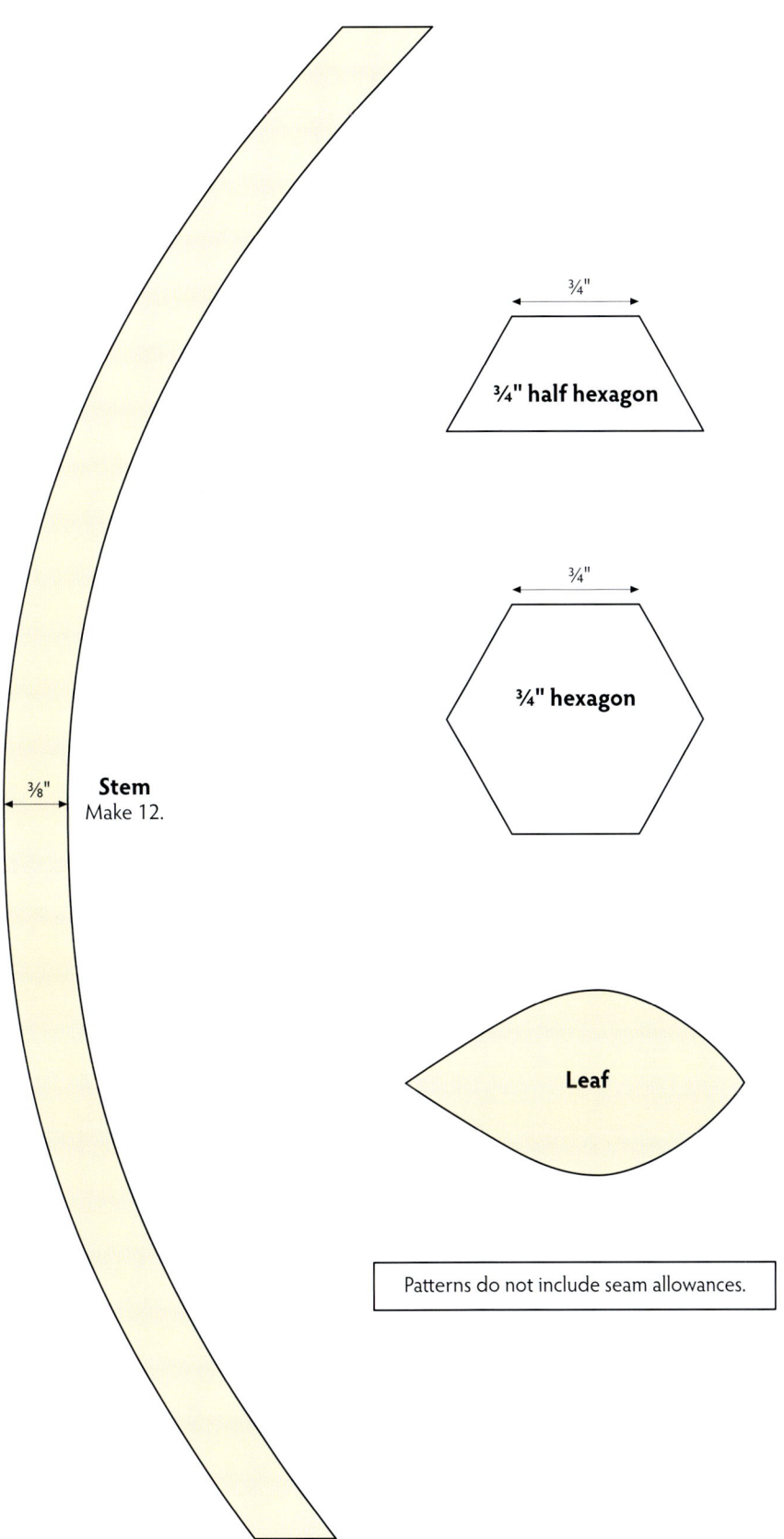

Summer Garden Bed Runner

How often do we neatly fold a quilt and place it at the foot of a bed as an accent, never to really see the full quilt? A bed runner seems to be a good alternative and takes a fraction of the time to make! I have a white matelassé coverlet on a bed in my own home and have begun to make an assortment of bed runners that I can easily change for a new look or a seasonal accent. I enjoy the variety these add to the room decor, and they make great gifts!

FINISHED BED RUNNER: 59½" x 26½"

Materials

Yardage is based on 42"-wide fabric.

1½ yards of large-scale floral for outer border
1½ yards of white solid for background
½ yard of multicolored stripe for scallops and binding
2 fat quarters *each* of pink, yellow, blue, and green prints or solids for flower petals and leaves
¼ yard of green tone on tone for stems and inner border
24 large flower petal papers, 4"
18 small flower petal papers, 3"
8 large leaf papers, 6"
12 small leaf papers, 2¾"
17 scallop papers, 3"
4 large hexagon papers, 1"
3 small hexagon papers, ¾"
2 yards of fabric for backing
31" x 64" piece of batting
Appliqué glue and freezer paper **OR** ⅓ yard of lightweight fusible web, 18" wide

Cutting

Refer to "English Paper Piecing" on page 5 for cutting flower petals, leaves, scallops, and hexagons; baste all shapes to the papers. Refer to "Quiltmaking Basics" on page 9 to prepare the stems for appliqué. Patterns are on page 49.

From the 2 blues and 2 pinks, cut:
6 large flower petals *from each*
3 pink scallops *total*
2 blue scallops *total*
3 small hexagons *total*

From the 2 yellows, cut:
9 small flower petals *from each*
3 scallops *total*
4 large hexagons *total*

From *each* of the 2 greens, cut:
4 large leaves
6 small leaves

From the green tone on tone, cut:
7 stems
2 strips, 2½" x 42"

From the white solid, cut on the *lengthwise* grain:
1 strip, 17½" x 54"

From the multicolored stripe, cut:
9 scallops
5 strips, 2" x 42"

From the large-scale floral, cut on the *lengthwise* grain:
3 strips, 4½" x 54"; crosscut into 2 strips, 4½" x 51½", and 2 strips, 4½" x 26½"

Making the Flowers

1. Whipstitch six large pink petals together, three from each pink print, to form one large flower. Begin stitching at the narrow inside point and stitch upward approximately 1¾". Make two pink flowers. Repeat to make two blue flowers using three large petals from each of the blue prints.

Make 2 of each.

2. Repeat step 1 using six small yellow petals, three of each yellow. Stitch from the center upward approximately 1⅜". Make three yellow flowers.

Assembling the Bed Runner

1. Whipstitch the 17 assorted scallops together along the side edges. Press well on both sides; remove basting and paper pieces.

2. Center the scallop strip on the 17½" x 54" white rectangle, aligning the bottom raw edges. Pin in place along the bottom edge. Arrange the large and small flowers, the stems, and the large and small leaves onto the white rectangle as shown, tucking the stems behind the scallops and trimming them as needed.

Summer Garden Bed Runner

Summer Garden Bed Runner

3. Appliqué the flowers, leaves, and stems in place by hand or machine. Add the hexagon flower centers and appliqué them to the flowers.

4. Hand or machine appliqué the scallop strip along the top curved edges.

5. Trim the appliquéd rectangle along the sides and top to measure 16½" x 51½". There should be ¼" on each end of the scallop strip for seam allowances.

6. With right sides together, stitch the 2½" green tone-on-tone strips together end to end at a 45° angle and trim to measure 51½". Stitch this strip to the bottom of the appliquéd rectangle.

7. Stitch the 4½" x 51½" floral strips to the top and bottom of the bed runner, pressing seam allowances toward the border. Stitch a 4½" x 26½" floral strip to each side and press.

Finishing

Refer to page 12 for details on marking, layering, basting, and quilting your project. Then use the 2"-wide striped strips to bind the bed runner.

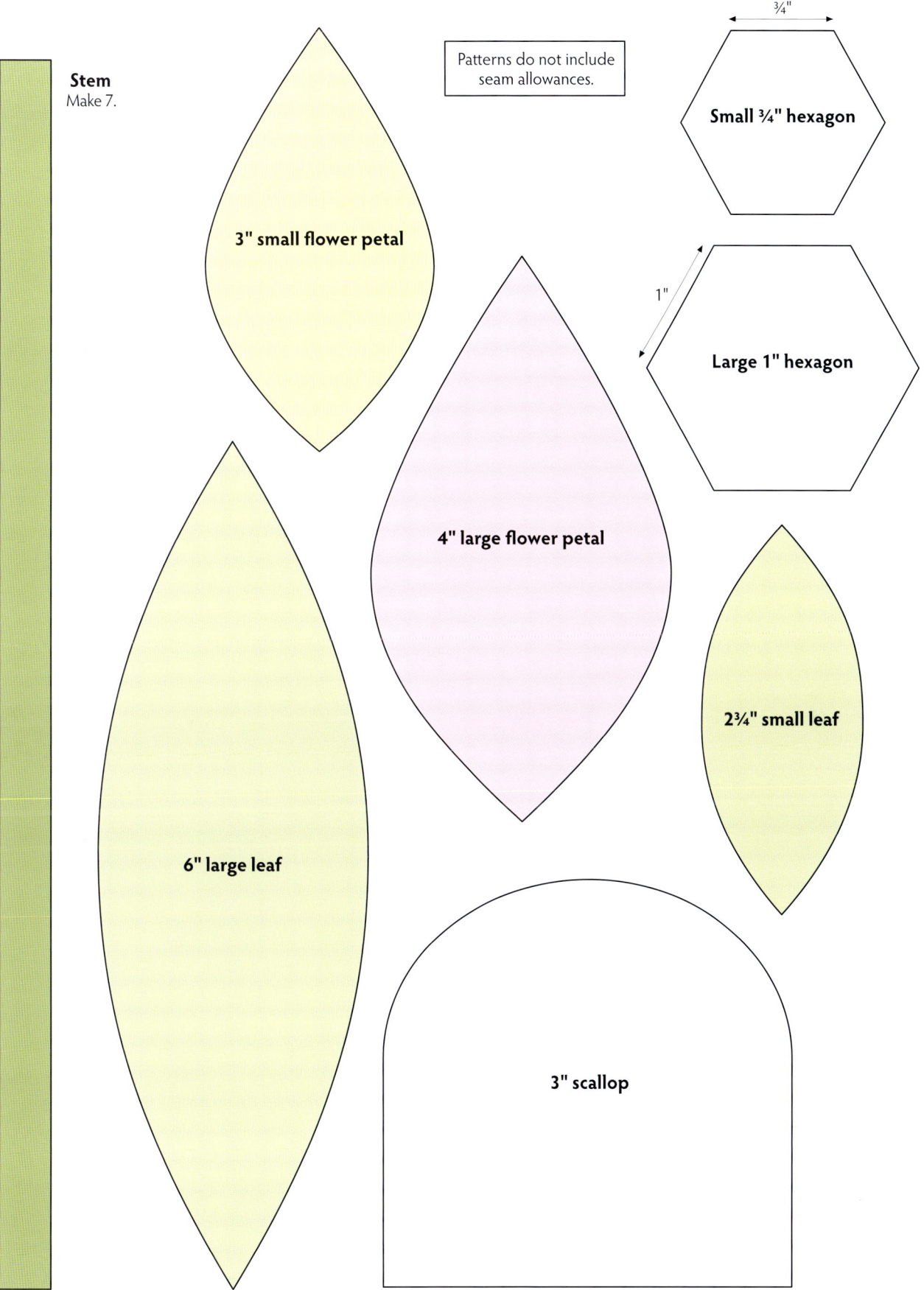

Summer Garden Bed Runner

Just Judie Goes Miniature

One of my favorite quilts in English Paper Piecing was "Just Judie," which was a tribute to my friend Judie Rothermel. Because Judie is known for her miniature quilts, I decided to make a small version of the quilt using a variety of Judie's Civil War reproduction fabrics I've collected over the years. This is an ideal project for small scraps!

Finished quilt: 13" x 17"

Materials

Yardage is based on 42"-wide fabric.

⅜ yard of light muslin for diamonds and border
1 fat quarter of dark green print for vines
160 squares, 1½" x 1½", of assorted medium to dark prints for hexagons
84 squares, 1¼" x 1¼", of assorted medium to dark prints for leaves and starflowers
¼ yard of dark floral for binding
1 fat quarter of fabric for backing
15" x 19" piece of batting
160 hexagon papers, ½"
219 papers for 6-point diamonds, ½"
18 equilateral triangle papers, ½"
Size 7, 8, or 9 Sharp needle and thread to match fabric
Appliqué glue
4 miniature red buttons, ¼" diameter
Wave Edge ruler (optional)
¼" bias press bar

Cutting

Refer to "English Paper Piecing" on page 5 for cutting hexagons, diamonds, and triangles; baste all shapes to the papers. Refer to "Making Bias Vines" on page 11 to cut and prepare the vines for appliqué. Patterns are on page 54.

From the assorted medium to dark prints, cut:
160 hexagons
84 diamonds

From the light muslin, cut:
2 strips, 2¼" x 42"
135 diamonds
18 triangles

From the dark green print, cut:
¾" bias strips to total approximately 75"

From the dark floral, cut:
2 strips, 2" x 42"

Making the Quilt Top

1. Whipstitch 16 assorted hexagons together to make one vertical row.

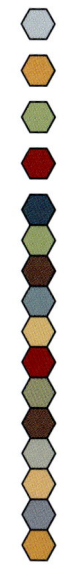

2. The next vertical row will begin with a light triangle, followed by 15 light diamonds and ending with a light triangle. Whipstitch each of these to the hexagon row as shown.

3. Continue making and adding hexagon rows and diamond rows until you have a total of 10 hexagon rows and nine diamond rows. The basting and paper pieces can be removed as you continue to add rows. However, be sure to leave the papers in the first and last pieces of each row and in the side rows until the entire quilt center is finished.

4. Press the quilt well on both sides and remove all of the papers.

Just Judy Goes Miniature

5. Draw a line on both sides of the quilt through the center of the outer hexagon rows. Stay stitch on the drawn line. Trim the sides of the quilt ¼" beyond the drawn line.

Adding the Border

Measure your quilt before cutting the border strips and make adjustments as needed.

1. Cut two 2¼" x 9½" strips from the light muslin strips for the top and bottom borders. Using a water-soluble marking pen and a Wave Edge ruler (or make a template using the wave pattern on page 54), draw a curved line down the center of each strip.

2. With the vine extending 2" beyond each end of the border, apply a few drops of appliqué glue to the wrong side of the vine and glue baste onto the curved line as you move down the border. Leave approximately 2" of vine unglued at the ends of each border strip and in addition to the 2" extending off each end.

3. Evenly space 11 medium to dark diamonds along the vine, glue baste in place, and machine or hand appliqué the vines and leaves to the border. Make two of these borders and sew to the top and bottom of the quilt.

Make 2.

4. Cut two 2¼" x 17½" strips from the remaining light muslin strip. Repeat steps 1 and 2, but do not include the extra 2" of vine.

5. Evenly space 19 medium to dark diamonds on each side border, glue baste in place, and hand or machine appliqué to the border. Sew a border to each side of the quilt.

6. Whipstitch six medium to dark diamonds together to make one starflower. Press well, and then remove basting and pop out the paper pieces. Make four.

Make 4.

7. Position a starflower on each corner of the quilt. Curve the excess vine to go under the starflower and glue baste in place. Hand or machine appliqué to the quilt.

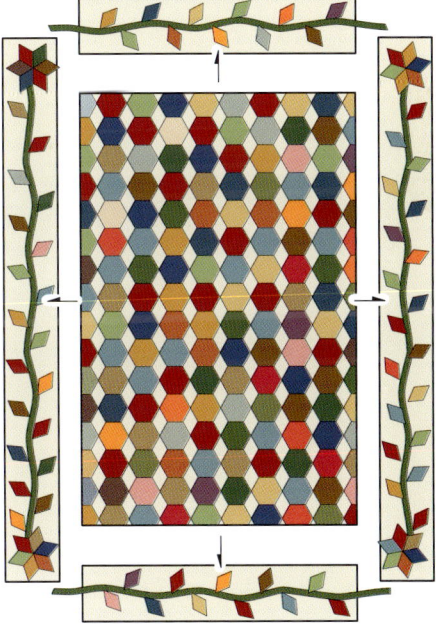

Finishing

1. Refer to page 12 for details on marking, layering, basting, and quilting your project. Then use the 2"-wide dark floral strips to bind the quilt.

2. Hand sew a small button in the center of each starflower.

Just Judie Goes Miniature

Wave pattern

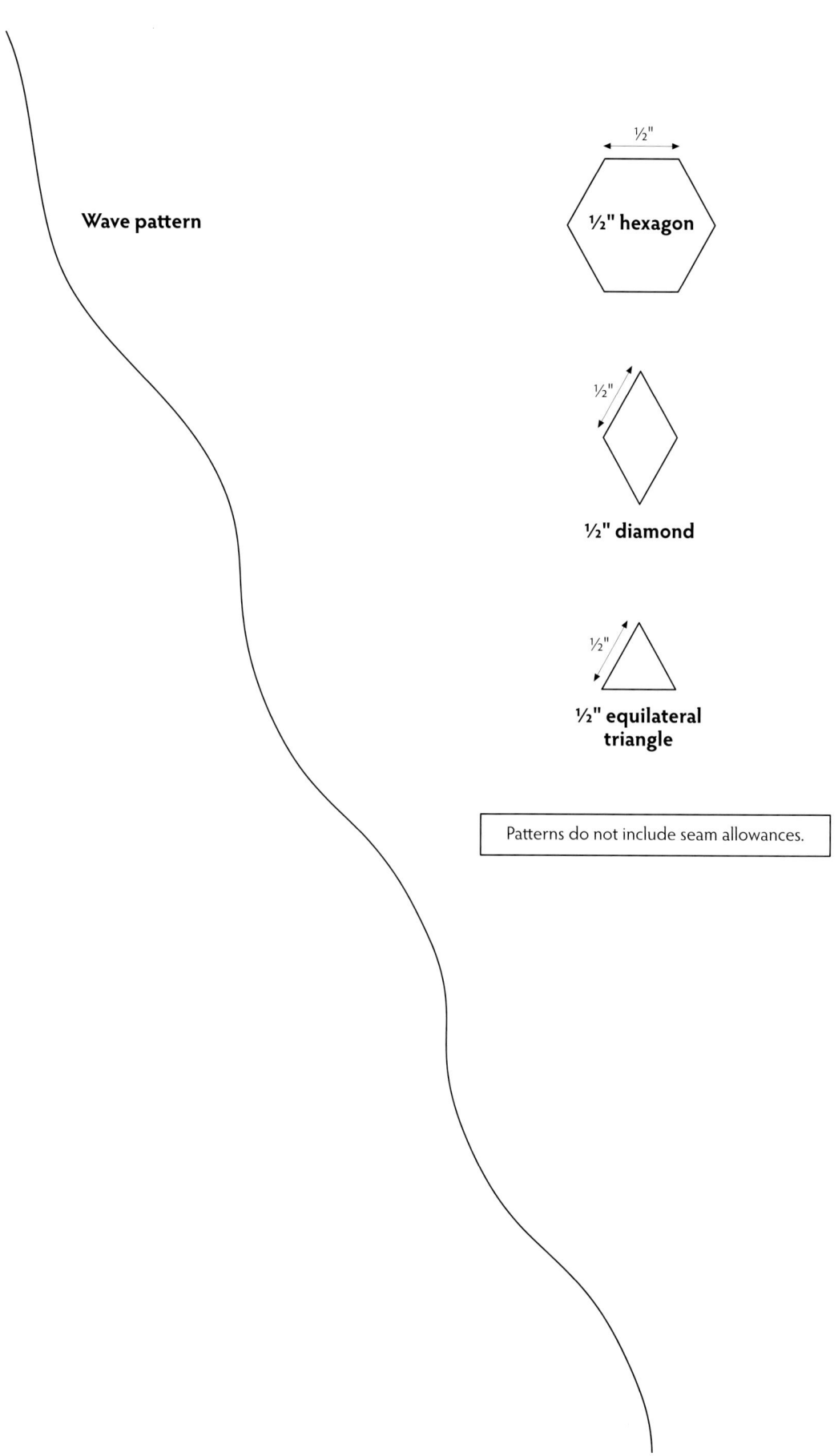

½"
½" hexagon

½"
½" diamond

½"
½" equilateral triangle

Patterns do not include seam allowances.

Flower Garden Tote

Because I always take an English-paper-piecing project with me whenever I travel or go to quilt group, I decided to make a tote for carrying my supplies. With two pockets on the inside, this bag has room for everything I need, and the fact that it's English paper pieced is so appropriate for what I'm using it for!

FINISHED TOTE: 13½" x 12½" x 4"

Materials

Yardage is based on 42"-wide fabric; charm squares measure 5" x 5".

1⅜ yards of black-and-tan print for hexagons, lining, pockets, and binding

1¼ yards* of border stripe for tote exterior and lining

25 assorted red-print charm squares for hexagons**

25 assorted brown-print charm squares for hexagons**

1¼ yards of fusible fleece, such as Thermolam, 36" wide***

1 pair of 18" black leather handles

528 hexagon papers, ½"

Size 7, 8, or 9 Sharp needles and thread to match fabric

Heavyweight thread (pearl cotton or quilting thread)

Yardage is based on a lengthwise stripe.

**Or you may substitute 7 assorted fat eighths.*

***Fusible fleece is stiffer than regular batting and gives the tote extra body.*

Cutting

Refer to "English Paper Piecing" on page 5 for cutting hexagons; baste all hexagons to the papers. Pattern is on page 58.

From the assorted red prints, cut:
15 matching sets of 6 hexagons
2 matching sets of 4 hexagons
17 hexagons

From the assorted brown prints, cut:
15 matching sets of 6 hexagons
2 matching sets of 4 hexagons
17 hexagons

From the black-and-tan print, cut:
1 strip, 4½" x 38¼"
1 rectangle, 14" x 19"
3 strips, 2½" x 42"
298 hexagons

From the border stripe, cut on the *lengthwise* grain:
2 strips, 2½" x 14" (with identical stripe placement)
1 strip, 4½" x 38¼"
2 rectangles, 13" x 14"

From the fusible fleece, cut:
2 rectangles, 13" x 14"
1 strip, 4½" x 38¼"

Making the Tote Front and Back

1. Whipstitch six matching red hexagons to a brown center hexagon to form a hexagon flower. Make 15. Whipstitch four matching red hexagons to a brown center to form a partial flower. Make two. Repeat, reversing the red and brown hexagons to make 15 matching flowers and two partial flowers.

  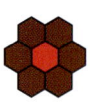

Make 15.　　Make 2.　　Make 15.　　Make 2.

2. Whipstitch the black-and-tan hexagons around the flowers as shown for the tote front. Repeat for the back, alternating the placement of the red and brown flowers.

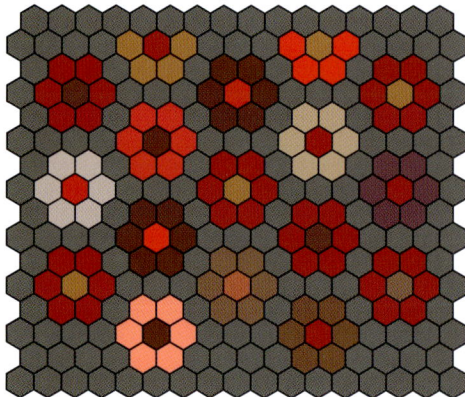

Front

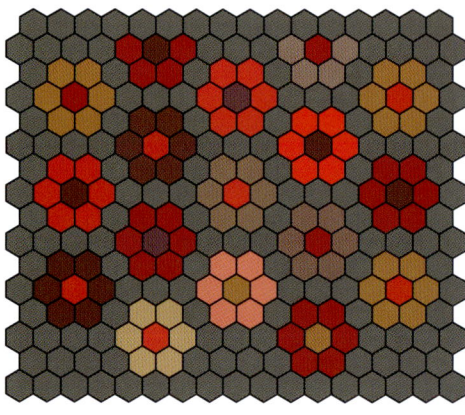

Back

3. Press the tote front and back well on both sides and remove the basting and paper pieces. Draw cutting lines around the tote front and back to measure 11" x 14" as shown. Stitch around all four sides of the tote front and back just inside the drawn line to reinforce the whipstitching before cutting. Using a rotary cutter, trim all four sides on the drawn line.

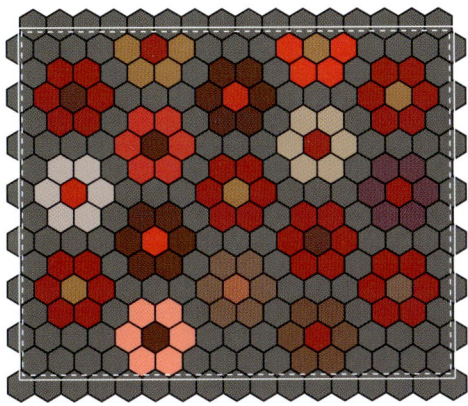

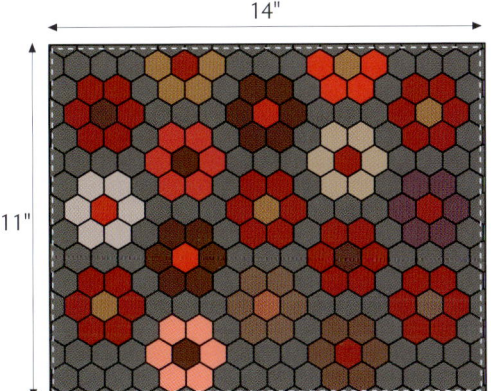

4. With right sides together, stitch a 2½" x 14" striped piece to the top of the tote front, and repeat for the back, pressing seam allowances toward the stripe.

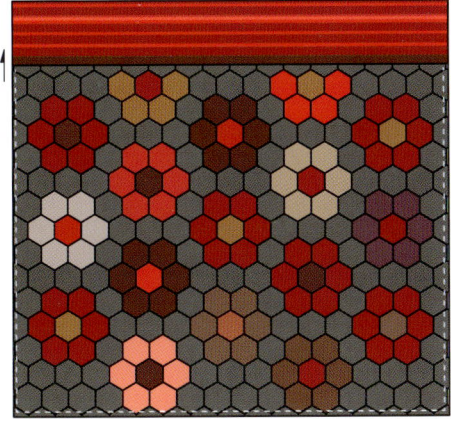

5. Lay each 13" x 14" piece of fusible fleece on the wrong side of a 13" x 14" striped lining piece. Lay the tote front and back onto the fusible fleece, right side up. Fuse the fleece following the manufacturer's instructions. Hand or machine quilt if desired. Repeat with the 4½" x 38¼" strips of border stripe, black-and-tan print, and fusible fleece for the sides and bottom of the tote.

6. Fold the 14" x 19" black-and-tan rectangle in half, wrong sides together, to make a pocket unit measuring 14" x 9½". Topstitch ¼" from the folded top edge.

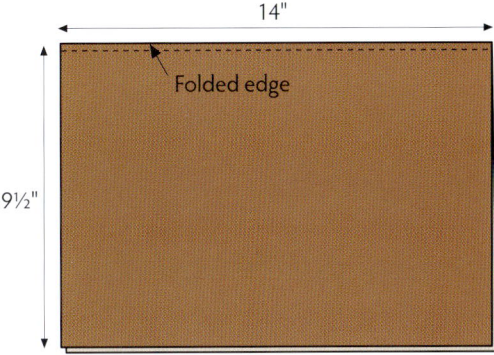

7. Place the pocket unit onto the right side of one of the 13" x 14" lining pieces, aligning the bottom and side raw edges. Baste in place around the outer edges, and then topstitch down the middle of the pocket through all layers to create two pockets. Backstitch at the upper edge to reinforce the pocket openings.

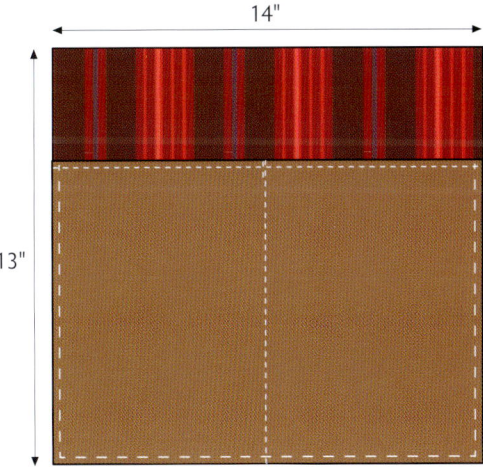

8. Make a paper template using the corner pattern on page 58, and trim the bottom corners of the tote front and back.

Flower Garden Tote 57

Assembling the Tote

1. Pin together and stitch the prepared tote front to the 4½" x 38¼" strip for the sides and bottom, having right sides together and easing in fullness at corners.

2. Pin and sew the tote back to the remaining edge of the strip.

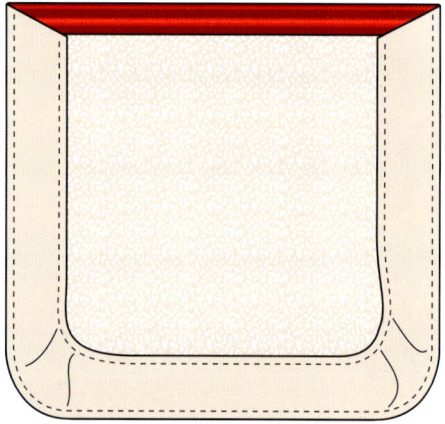

Finishing

1. With wrong sides together, fold the 2½"-wide black-and-tan strips in half and press. Bind the gusset seams on the inside of the tote and then the raw top edge of the tote. (Refer to "Binding the Quilt" on page 13 as needed.)

2. Center the ends of the black leather handles onto the front and back of the tote and hand stitch in place using a strong thread such as quilting thread or pearl cotton.

EASY-BASTE HANDLES
To keep the handles secure while you are hand stitching them to the tote, staple them in place and then remove the staples after the hand stitching is complete.

½"

½" hexagon

Pattern does not include seam allowances.

Corner pattern

English Paper Piecing II

Indigo Stars

Several years ago I was rummaging through a trunk filled with keepsakes, when I came across a quilt that my Great Aunt Wilma had stitched for me by hand as a wedding gift. The blocks in my wedding quilt were cross-stitched stars, stems, and leaves and the overall effect was beautiful! I was inspired to re-create this quilt incorporating English paper piecing and appliqué in lieu of the cross-stitch.

Finished quilt: 48" x 48"
Finished block: 16" x 16"

Materials

Yardage is based on 42"-wide fabric.

2 yards of light print for blocks, sashing, and outer border
½ yard of gold print for appliqués, sashing squares, and inner border
4 fat quarters of assorted dark blue prints for appliqués
2 fat quarters of assorted gold prints for appliqués and sashing squares
1 fat quarter of blue-and-gold print for sashing squares and border corner squares
⅛ yard of pewter print for stems
½ yard of blue-and-gold stripe for binding
3 yards of fabric for backing
53" x 53" piece of batting
32 papers for 8-point diamonds, 3"
4 square papers, 2"
Size 7, 8, or 9 Sharp needle and thread to match fabric
Appliqué glue and freezer paper **OR** 1¼ yards of lightweight fusible web, 18" wide

Cutting

Refer to "English Paper Piecing" on page 5 for cutting diamonds and squares; baste all shapes to the papers. Refer to "Quiltmaking Basics" on page 9 to prepare the buds, leaves, and stems for appliqué. Patterns are on page 63.

From *each* of the 4 assorted dark-blue prints, cut:
4 diamonds
12 leaves

From *each* of the 2 gold print fat quarters, cut:
4 diamonds
12 buds
1 square, 2" x 2" (for paper piecing)
1 square, 2½" x 2½"

From the ½ yard of gold print, cut:
4 strips, 1½" x 42"; trim 2 strips to 38½" long and 2 strips to 40½" long
8 diamonds
24 buds
2 squares, 2" x 2" (for paper piecing)
2 squares, 2½" x 2½"

From the pewter print, cut:
16 stems

From the light print, cut:
2 strips, 16½" x 42"; crosscut into 4 squares, 16½" x 16½"
5 strips, 2½" x 42"; crosscut into 24 rectangles, 2½" x 7½"
4 strips, 4½" x 40½"

From the blue-and-gold print, cut:
3 strips, 2½" x 21"; crosscut into 17 squares, 2½" x 2½"
4 squares, 4½" x 4½"

From the blue-and-gold stripe, cut:
2"-wide bias strips to total 206"

Making the Flower Blocks

1. Whipstitch together four matching pairs of blue diamonds and gold diamonds. Make four for each block.

Make 4.

2. Lightly press each 16½" light square in half diagonally in both directions, and then in half vertically and horizontally to assist with the placement of the stems, center square, and diamond pairs. Use the creases to position the appliqués as shown on page 62. Appliqué all pieces in place by hand or machine,

Indigo Stars

making sure to leave at least ⅜" on all sides to allow for seam allowances. Make four blocks. **Note:** *You may remove the paper pieces prior to appliquéing the shapes if desired. This would eliminate the need to cut away the background fabric later.*

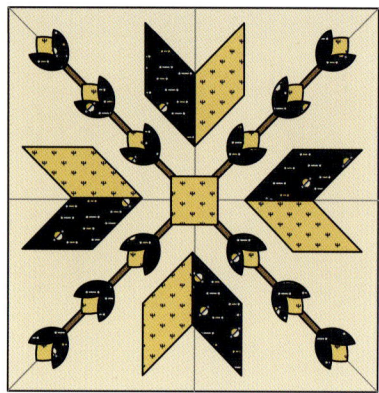

Make 4.

3. Turn each block over to the wrong side. Cut away the background fabric a generous ¼" to ½" inside the appliqué stitching and remove the paper pieces.

Assembling the Quilt Top

1. Stitch 2½" x 7½" light-print rectangles to opposite sides of a 2½" gold square. Press the seam allowances toward the rectangles. Make four of these units measuring 2½" x 16½". Repeat to make eight with 2½" blue-and-gold squares.

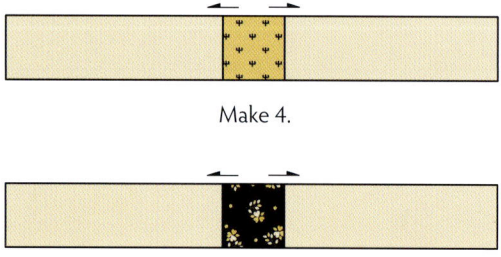

Make 4.

Make 8.

2. Arrange the blocks, sashing units, and the remaining 2½" blue-and-gold squares as shown. Sew the pieces into rows, pressing the seam allowances toward the sashing. Sew the rows together. The quilt should measure 38½" x 38½".

3. Stitch the 1½" x 38½" gold strips to the top and bottom of the quilt, pressing the seam allowances toward the gold print. Sew the 1½" x 40½" gold strips to the sides and press.

4. Stitch 4½" x 40½" light-print strips to the top and bottom of the quilt, pressing the seam allowances toward the light strips. Stitch a 4½" blue-and-gold square to each end of the remaining border strips, pressing the seam allowances toward the light print. Stitch one of these border strips to each side of the quilt and press.

Finishing

Refer to page 12 for details on marking, layering, basting, and quilting your project. Then use the 2"-wide blue-and-gold bias strips to bind the quilt.

English Paper Piecing II

Stem
Make 16.

3" diamond

Bud

Leaf

Make 48 of each.

Patterns do not include seam allowances.

2" square

Indigo Stars

About the Author

Vicki Bellino lives in far northern California with her husband of 41 years, Danté. They have a daughter and a son and four granddaughters, ages 15, 13, 10 and 9. Danté and Vicki enjoy traveling and taking their grandchildren on RV trips to the California and Oregon coasts. Vicki has taught all of the girls to sew, and they have finished numerous quilts and tote bags and are often found helping Vicki with many of the tasks related to her quilting business.

Vicki has been quilting for nearly 30 years and has been an avid English paper piecer since learning the technique over six years ago. This is her second English-paper-piecing book with Martingale and she has incorporated EPP into many of her patterns, as well. This book gave Vicki the opportunity to incorporate English paper piecing into a variety of projects that had been in her design file for quite some time.

Vicki is one of those people who is happiest when her hands are busy, which is one of the reasons she is so passionate about English paper piecing! She keeps a basket of fabric scraps and paper pieces next to her favorite chair and is always either basting or whipstitching while watching television with her husband in the evening. She takes an EPP project with her nearly everywhere she goes and teaches the technique to anyone who is interested!

What's your creative passion?

Find it at ShopMartingale.com

books • eBooks • ePatterns • daily blog • free projects
videos • tutorials • inspiration • giveaways